Harriet Trubee Knapp Garlick

History of the Trubee Family

Harriet Trubee Knapp Garlick

History of the Trubee Family

ISBN/EAN: 9783337143831

Printed in Europe, USA, Canada, Australia, Japan

Cover: Foto ©ninafisch / pixelio.de

More available books at **www.hansebooks.com**

MRS. SAMUEL M. GARLICK.
(HARRIET TRUBEL KNAPP.)

1275.   1894.

History

of the

Trubee Family,

BY

HARRIET TRUBEE GARLICK.

BRIDGEPORT, CONN.:
PUBLISHED BY THE MARIGOLD PRINTING COMPANY.
1894.

Affectionately dedicated to the memory of my beloved grandfather Samuel Comfort Trubee.

                Harriet Trubee Garlick.

INTRODUCTION.

Realizing the fact, that unless the members of a family are sufficiently interested in their past record to preserve it in writing, it will be forgotten and lost by the passing away of generation after generation, I have written, for the benefit of ourselves and descendants, a history of our family, commencing with our Hebrew ancestor Andris Trubee, of Holland.

The Jews of that land came from Spain; where, for many years, they had occupied the highest positions in literature, art and wealth. In order to escape persecution many of the Jews, outwardly, embraced Catholicism, but secretly worshiped the "God of Israel."

King Ferdinand and Queen Isabella resolved to confiscate the property of their Jewish population for the benefit of the Church and State; therefore they issued a manifesto expelling all Hebrews within their realm. Noblemen and peasants were treated with the same severity, and soon beautiful homes and halls of learning, were vacated for the crowded vessel, and a refuge in a strange land; penniless, and with only a few articles of clothing, many of this abused people reached Holland, where their industrious habits soon enabled them to acquire, again, a competency.

Andris Trubee descended from these Spanish refugees.

CONTENTS.

HISTORICAL.

INTRODUCTION.

	PAGE.
Andris Trubee,	13
Ansel Trubee,	29
David Trubee,	39
Samuel Comfort Trubee,	43
Samuel Curtiss Trubee;	75
William Trubee,	79
Andrew Trubee,	85
James Staples,,	89

GENEALOGICAL.

Adams,	93
Beach,	99
Beers,	97
Bennett,	99
Bishop,	96
Booth,	100
Bulkley,	110

CONTENTS.

	PAGE
CRANE,	113
CURTISS,	115
GARLICK,	118
GIBNEY,	121
HOILE,	121
KNAPP,	122
MILLER,	128
PERRY,	128
SANFORD,	129
SOMERS,	129
STAPLES,	140
TRUBEE,	133
TURNEY,	130
WELLS,	144
WRIGHT,	147

INDEX.

	PAGE
ADAMS,	93
ABIGAIL,	15, 19, 95
ABRAHAM,	16, 17, 18, 95
ABRAHAM 2ND,	96
SAMUEL,	18, 19, 20, 30, 94
SAMUEL, 2ND,	19
DANIEL,	19
SAMUEL,	30, 31
ALDEN, ADA,	83
ALVORD, JESSOP,	81
SUSAN,	81
BANKS, EDWIN,	15
BASSETT, GOODY,	85
BALDWIN, SAMUEL,	83
MARY,	83
BARLOW, JOHN,	29
BEACH, JOHN,	99
ABIAH,	53
BETHIA,	52
BENNETT, CHARLES,	73, 99

INDEX.

	PAGE
BISHOP, ALFRED,	82
HENRY A.,	82
JOHN,	82
WILLIAM D.,	81
BOOTH GENEALOGICAL,	100–109
ASSOCIATION,	50
BETHIA,	48
GIDEON,	49
NICHOLAS,	50
CHARLES,	49–50
WILLIAM,	49–52
RICHARD,	48, 49, 51, 52
SARAH,	49
BULKLEY GENEALOGY,	110
BULKLAUGH, LORD,	29
GERSHOM,	29
BULKLEY, PETER,	29, 30
BURR, DAVID,	22, 23, 24, 25
COLEY, JONATHAN,	25
CHAUNCEY, ROBERT,	21
CLAWSON, ELIZABETH,	17
CRANE, GENEALOGY.	113–114
CURTISS, MARTHA,	39
ELIZABETH,	47
WILLIAM,	47–49
GENEALOGY,	115–117
DAVISON, HARRY,	83
DOAN, ELISHA,	84, 137
SUSAN,	84, 138

INDEX.

	PAGE
DISBROUGH,	17
ELLIOTT, REV. ANDREW,	34
GARLICK, SAMUEL, 1ST,	119
JOHN,	64, 119
DR. SAMUEL,	63–65, 120
GIBNEY, ALEXANDER,	121
VIRGIL, DR.,	82, 83, 121
HOILE, GEORGE,	59, 121
ROBERT,	59, 121
HANCOCK, JOHN,	30, 31
JUDSON, WILLIAM,	52–54
KNAPP, EZRA,	34
JOHN,	59
RUFUS, 1ST,	59–64
RUFUS, 2ND,	60–65
WILLIAM,	66–73
HERBERT,	65
GENEALOGY,	122–127
LIVESLEY, ELIZABETH,	29
MILLER,	17, 128
NEWTON, THOMAS,	16
PERRY,	73, 128
QUINCY, DOROTHY,	30
STAPLES,	17, 85, 140–144
SAMUEL,	35
JAMES,	89–91
SHELTON, REV. PHILO,	34
TRUBEE, ANDRIS,	14–29, 133
ANSEL,	29–39

INDEX.

	PAGE
TRUBEE, DAVID, . .	39–42
SAMUEL COMFORT,	43–74
SAMUEL CURTISS,	75–78
WILLIAM, . .	79–85
WILLIAM EDGAR,	81
WILLIAM ALVORD, . .	83
SAMUEL CURTISS, 2ND,	83
FREDERICK, . .	83
ANDREW, .	85–89
GENEALOGY, .	133–140
TURNEY, CAPTAIN AARON,	32
BENJAMIN, .	130–132
ABEL, .	60
WELLS, . . .	144–147
WRIGHT, .	72, 147

INDEX TO ILLUSTRATIONS.

	OPPOSITE PAGE
ADAMS COAT-OF-ARMS,	93
ANDRIS TRUBEE'S BRASS BOX,	13
BOOTH COAT-OF-ARMS,	100
BULKLEY COAT-OF-ARMS,	110
BULKLEY TAVERN,	32
CURTISS COAT-OF-ARMS,	115
GARLICK, SAMUEL MIDDLETON, M. D.,	118
MRS. SAMUEL M., (HARRIET TRUBEE KNAPP,)	OP. TITLE PAGE
HOILE, GEORGE,	57
MRS. GEORGE, (ELIZABETH TRUBEE),	59
KNAPP, CAPTAIN RUFUS,	60
MRS. RUFUS, (CAROLINE TRUBEE),	63
RUFUS CLIFTON,	126
CAPTAIN WILLIAM,	66
MRS. WILLIAM, (HARRIET TRUBEE),	72
HERBERT MERTON,	65
MILLER, ZEPHENIAH,	131
MRS. ZEPHENIAH, (JANE ANN TRUBEE),	133
ARTHUR MILLS,	128
STAPLES, FRANK,	140

INDEX TO ILLUSTRATIONS.

	OPPOSITE PAGE
STAPLES, JAMES,	89
MRS. JAMES, (SARAH ELIZABETH TRUBEE),	90
SOMERS, FREDERICK,	129
MRS. FREDERICK, (FRANCES HOILE),	121
TRUBEE HOMESTEAD,	53
TRUBEE, ANDREW,	85
MRS. ANDREW, (SARAH TURNEY),	86
CHARLOTTE,	135
DAVID, (1ST),	39
DAVID, (2ND),	84
MRS. DAVID, (MARTHA CURTISS),	40
FRANK,	139
FREDERICK,	83
SAMUEL COMFORT,	43
MRS. SAMUEL COMFORT, (ELIZABETH CURTISS),	47
SAMUEL CURTISS, (1ST),	75
SAMUEL CURTISS, (2ND),	138
WILLIAM,	79
MRS. WILLIAM, (ELIZA ANN KNAPP),	81
WILLIAM EDGAR,	83
WILLIAM ALVORD,	137
WRIGHT, JOHN WINTHROP, M. D.,	147

TRANSLATION.

JEREMIAH 9TH CHAPTER, 21ST VERSE.

"For death is come up into our windows and is entered into our palaces, to cut off our children from without, and the young men from the streets."

In the Inventory of Andris Trubee's Estate, 1759, is mentioned "1 brass snuff box."

This box is now in the possession of his great great granddaughter, Mrs. Frederick Somers, of Bridgeport; it must have been brought by Mr. Trubee from Holland late in the 17th or early in the 18th century.

The engraving on the cover of the box is beautifully reproduced in fac simile upon this page, and illustrates Jeremiah's prophecy concerning the children of Israel before their captivity in Babylon.

The cover of the box is of brass; the sides are of copper, illustrated with a hunting scene; on the left side is a tree, near it is a huge boar held at bay by a dog, whose master is about to shoot the animal with an Arquebus; this weapon was invented in 1485, and was fired by applying a "spunk" or match while resting it against the chest; on the opposite side are two hunting dogs evidently following the game.

The writing is in Dutch.

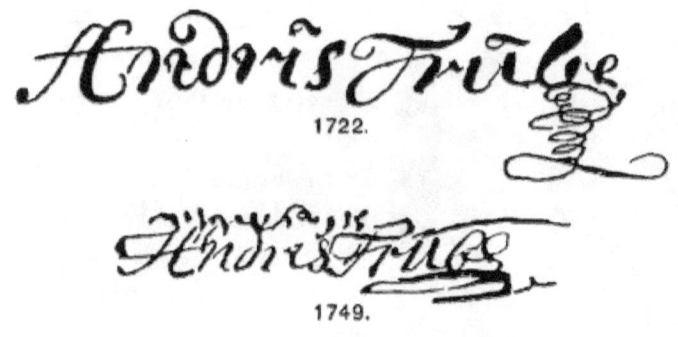

ANDRIS TRUBEE came from Holland to America in the latter part of 1600 or early in 1700. He first settled in Boston, where he entered into partnership with a Mr. Solomon. Being desirous of enlarging and extending their business, they opened a house furnishing store in Fairfield, Conn. It was situated on the north side of the main street nearly opposite the Rowland homestead. Mr. Trubee became resident manager.

At that time the town was one of importance; for it was the county seat, and contained a Court House, Jail, an Episcopal and Congregational church, fifteen stores, and several mills and factories.

Mr. Trubee was a man of intellectual attainments; understanding several languages, possessing an agreeable presence and rare conversational powers, his society was sought by the learned, though he was of the Hebrew faith. A number of Episcopal clergymen realizing how much assistance a man of his attainments could render their church, resolved by prayer and persuasion to bring him into the fold of the true Shepherd. Their efforts were successful, and Andris Trubee became a Christian; uniting with the Episcopal church which stood in the center of the present park at Mill Plain.

Mr. Trubee bought his goods at Boston and at Hartford. While at the latter place, in 1722, he signed his name as a witness to a business transaction of his friend Mr. Gold, of Fairfield. This autograph has lately been taken from the archives at Hartford; and the name so beautifully written by our ancestor one hundred and seventy-one years ago, we reverently place at the head of this chapter.

Mr. Trubee was twice married, his first wife's name was, probably, Abigail. Their daughter, Eunice, was born July 11th, 1740. Unfortunately for the historian the Episcopal church of which he was a member was destroyed by fire and its records were consumed; we are therefore unable to give the dates of his marriage and his wife's death, which must have occurred soon after the birth of her child, as he married his second wife, Abigail, daughter of Elijah and Abigail Adams Crane, April 14th, 1744. She was a descendant of Edward Adams, who came to New Haven in 1640, to Milford 1646, and to Fairfield 1650.

The statement that Edward Adams was of the same family as they of Presidential fame has been transmitted from generation to generation in the Adams family. I have been unable to find any written record of the fact, for time has hidden this unwritten history behind a cloud too dense to penetrate. Research may sometime find documents which will settle the relationship beyond doubt. The friendship between the Adams family of Massachusetts and they of Fairfield was continued as late, at least, as 1825, when John Q. Adams while traveling through this county on his way to take the Presidential chair, visited Miss Abigail Adams, of Green's Farms, who was an aunt of Mr. Edwin Banks, of Bridgeport. Our historical knowledge of the early settlers is very limited; they were too engrossed with the stern realities of life to write its records. Hardships, trials and dangers, were cheerfully endured by those pioneers who sought freedom and religious liberty. Through their sacrifices we have gained our freedom. Our ancester, Edward Adams, who came to this country to escape from the "Dragon of Persecution," bought of Andrew Ward, in 1650, the farm west of Hyde's Pond in Fairfield; after residing there a short time he purchased land at Barlow's Plain, where he removed and resided many years.

The laws of that time were very rigid; every man was obliged by law to carry his loaded gun with him to the field and to the sanctuary, and a fine was imposed if this precaution against the wiles of the savages was omitted. The Sabbath commenced at sundown Saturday evening, and closed at the same hour Sunday, when neighbors and friends congregated at each others houses, the men to smoke their clay pipes, and the women to gossip over their knitting. No one was allowed to ride on Sunday unless it was necessary in order to attend Divine service.

The penalty for firing a building was, death by hanging. A whipping-post upon the village green was the transgressor's dread; for there all minor offenses were punished with the lash. Thomas Newton had been fined £5 for giving a man wine, upon the vessel of which he was commander, when he was already intoxicated. Thomas Staples, Edward Adams, and four others, aided him in escaping to the Dutch, for which they were fined; Mr. Staples £40, and the others £20, which sum was remitted with the exception of the first mentioned gentleman, who was obliged to pay £20, as he was the originator of the scheme.

Edward Adams, by prudence and perseverance, became a large land owner, and when he died about 1671, left his widow and children "a goodly heritage."

To his son Abraham he gave a farm at Barlow's Plain; (it is now owned by Miss Elizabeth Morehouse); he and his wife Sarah had a large family, who were baptized in the Congregational church; he uniting with it December 9th, 1694.

Throughout the States, in 1692, there was an epidemic of hysteria, accompanied by strange hallucinations attributed to the machinations of the evil one, who taking possession of a few feeble minded women gave them power to ride on broomsticks and enter the windows of the sick; where sitting on the footboards of their beds they leered and made faces, and by pinching and pricking them caused much distress of mind and body.

In 1692 Goody Disbrough, Clawson, Miller and Staples were arrested as witches in Fairfield, and were tried for complicity with Satan; the two latter named were acquitted, but the two former were found guilty, and were condemned to pass through the ordeal of trial by water. This penalty was inflicted by tying the prisoners hands and feet together and throwing them into a pond—if they sank they were pronounced innocent, but if they floated they were guilty and worthy of death. The testimony of Abraham Adams and Jonathan Squires is, that when Mary Disbrough and Elizabeth Clawson were bound hand and foot and put into the water, "They swam like cork and one laboured to press them into the water, and they buoyed up like cork." Sworn in Court September 1st, 1692. It is not supposed these women suffered capital punishment as a Mrs. Disbrough lived at Westport many years after this event.

On Thanksgiving Day, November 10th, 1725, the Episcopal church on Mill Plain green, was dedicated amid the general rejoicing of its members. Abraham Adams, one of its founders, and a most liberal contributor towards its support, died August 9th, 1728, aged 80 years, and was buried in its church-yard. In 1735 this primitive building was replaced by one 55 feet by 35 feet in size and 20 feet high, with a handsome steeple and spire of 100 feet in height, and a good bell of 500 pounds weight. This edifice was erected upon the land where Mr. Emery Rowland's house now stands. In 1779 this church, with its valuable parish records, was destroyed by fire in the conflagration which desolated Fairfield. Upon the Mill Plain green, in 1780, a third church edifice was erected and Rev. Philo Shelton became its rector. He served the parish faithfully forty years, and died February 28th, 1825.

The church was rebuilt about 1840 in Southport, and the ground where it had been located converted into a public park; its church-yard was leveled; a few of its stones were removed and stored in Mr. Sturges' greenhouse until the centennial of the burning of Fairfield, when they were removed to the old cemetery on the beach lane and placed in a row with a new brown stone slab at their head; upon which was inscribed the names copied from the blue slate gravestones which had become too broken for their inscriptions to be easily deciphered. The first is "Abraham Adams, died 1728."

Samuel Adams, son of Edward, was our ancestor. He inherited from his father the property west of Hyde's

Pond. It was retained in the family over two hundred years, when it was divided into building lots and sold.

Samuel Adams, by his wife Mary, had two sons, Samuel and Daniel. His wife died and he married Mary, daughter of Robert Meeker, by whom he had a large family. His daughter Abigail, our ancestress, was the wife of Elijah Crane; their daughter, Abigail, married Andris Trubee, of Fairfield. We have not the dates of Samuel Adams and several of his children's baptisms, because the Congregational church records only commence at 1694. We know they must necessarily have been baptized as it was then considered essential to salvation, and so important was it deemed, that an infant dying without receiving this seal of the New Covenant was considered lost. Many people joined the church at that time through the "Half-way Covenant," which read—

"You do now, before God and these witnesses, avouch the Lord Jehovah to be your covenant God and Father, viewing yourself under solemn bonds and obligations to be the Lord's by your baptismal vows. You do, so far as you know your own heart, make choice of Jesus Christ to be your only Saviour and Redeemer, and the Holy Ghost to be your Sanctifier, solemnly engaging to serve the Lord and him only, as he shall by his grace enable you; that you will deny all ungodliness and worldly lusts; that you will be careful to keep a conscience void of offence, so as to do honor to God and the religion you profess; that you will endeavor by strength from God to walk in all his commandments and ordinances blameless, desiring to put yourself under the watch and care of this church, to be trained up in the school of Christ for his heavenly kingdom ; promising also that you will give up to God your children in baptism, and to bring them up in the fear of the Lord ; and to attend upon all the ordinances of Christ as administered in this place ; also that it is your full purpose to obey God in the ordinance of the Holy Supper as God shall give you light, and show you his will herein. And you covenant, and you promise, relying for help, strength, and ability on the blood of the everlasting covenant to perform all and every duty to the praise and glory of God."

These solemn obligations soon led many of its members to enter into full membership with the church of Christ.

Samuel Adams died before 1720, but we have neither the exact record of his death nor of his place of interment; he and his children are a part of that past history of Fairfield of which so little has been written, but which has given to us, its children, our homes, our religion, and our liberty.

In the Maritime and Trade Affairs at Hartford, (1722, Vol. I., Document 85), we find the signature of Andris Trubee, again his name appears in the same volume, (Document 138); it is a memorial of the trades of Fairfield County to the General Assembly of 1749.

Andris Trubee must have been a man somewhat advanced in years when he married his second wife, as he was a business man in 1722. Eight children came to fill their home with mirth and joy. He and his family must have been baptized in the Episcopal church at Mill Plain with the exception of one daughter, Geerlow, who was baptized in the Congregational church.

Although a convert to the Christian faith, Mr. Trubee always retained the Jewish dislike for pork, but when called from home on business, his wife's table was plentifully supplied with this article.

In Book 11, page 97, 1752, Fairfield Records, there is an account of Andris Trubee buying a farm of eight acres of Robert Chauncey, for which he paid £229 current money of gold tenor, June 21st, 1751.

On December 5th, 1758, Andris Trubee being very ill, made his will, which reads—

"In the name of God, Amen. This 5th day of December, 1758, I, Andris Trubee, of the town and County of Fairfield, and Colony of Connecticut, being weak in body do make and ordain this my last will and testament. First. I order and direct that all my just debts and funeral charges shall be paid by my executors, out of my personal estate.

ITEM. I give and bequeath unto my beloved wife, Abigail, the sum of one hundred lbs., lawful money.

ITEM. I give and bequeath unto my two daughters, Eunice and Esther, that is to each of them, the sum of thirty lbs., lawful money.

ITEM. I give and bequeath unto my son, Samuel, the sum of twenty lbs., on account of his being my eldest son.

ITEM. All the residue and remainder of my estate, both real and personal, not herein before given away, I give and divide unto my five sons, Samuel, Ansel, Alexander, David and Comfort ; to them and their heirs forever ; to be equally divided between them.

FOURTHLY. I do hereby constitute, ordain, and appoint my friends Ralph Isaacs, of Norwalk, and David Burr, of Fairfield, to be executors of this my last Will and Testament; declaring this to be my last Will and Testament. In witness whereof I have hereunto set my hand and seal in Fairfield." (Day and date just above written). "ANDRIS TRUBEE.

Signed, sealed, published and promised by the said Andris Trubee to be his last Will and Testament in presence of Samuel Squires and Joe Bartram and Jeremiah Gould."

"True copy (test)."
Fairfield Record, page 541, December 5th, 1758.

Mr. Trubee only lived a few days after his will was made, for he died in December, 1758. By his death Fairfield lost one of its prominent business men; the church a worthy disciple, and his family a husband and father. An old resident of Fairfield has described Mr. Andris Trubee in nearly the following words:

"I remember well seeing Mr. Andris Trubee walking the streets of Fairfield leaning upon his gold headed cane ; he was a dignified, fine looking old gentleman, who always dressed in the fashion of the day, wearing a ruffled shirt, broadcloth coat and breeches, with gold shoe buckles and silks stockings."

"At a Court of Probate held in Fairfield January 2nd, 1759, Personally appeared Samuel Squires and Jeremiah Gold, and made solemn oath that they saw Andris Trubee sign and seal ye written instrument and heard him declare ye same to be his last Will and Testament, and that they subscribed as witnesses in ye presence of the testator and they saw Joseph Bartram ye other witness sign at the same time, and that they then judged the testator to be of disposing mind and memory."

(Test.)

"At the above court personally appeared Ralph Isaacs and David Burr to accept the trust of executors, and at the same time exhibited this will for probation, the same being proved, is by this court approved and ordered to be recorded."

Upon the 17th day of January, 1759, an inventory was taken of the effects of Andris Trubee, lately deceased; it occupies several pages of the Fairfield Records. In the inventory of the household effects I have copied only a few articles which I thought might be interesting for his descendants to read:

"1 large chest and drawers. 1 large box. 2 large wheelers. 1 gun. 1 barrelfull of pork. 1 bbl. amost full of beef. Taffety coat and breeches. Voyage to the South Seas. 1 Common Prayer Book. 1 large Bible. 1 chest with double spring lock. 1 Broadcloth snuff-colored coat, not finished. 1 Sagathea coat. 1 Great coat. Beaver hat and box. Black silk stockings. Holland shirts. Gold sleeve buttons, gold shirt buttons, and gold stock buckle."

The inventory of his store was very lengthy and uninteresting.

HISTORY OF THE TRUBEE FAMILY.

The follow receipts and appointment of guardian were copied from the Fairfield Records, page 541:

"Received of David Burr, one of the executors of the last will and testament of my late husband, Andris Trubee, deceased, the sum of ten pounds, 14/4, lawfull money, toward the sum given me in said will.

ABIGAIL TRUBEE."

Witness, Isabell Osborn.

"Received of David Burr, of Fairfield, one of the executors of the last will and testament of Andris Trubee, late of Fairfield, in moneys and moveables, the sum of seventy pounds, nine shillings, and nine pence, being part of the sum given me in said will in lieu of Dower. I say Red, January 3rd, 1760.

Received, signed and allowed by her, 1 gun and one wood bottle.

Witnesses, MR. SANFORD, OSBORNE, ABIGAIL TRUBEE.

"Received of David Burr, one of the executors of the last will and testament of Andris Trubee, late of Fairfield; the sum of thirteen pounds, one shilling and five pence, lawfull money, being the remainder of the legacy given to said Truby's wife, Abigail, in said will, which remained unpaid at her death. July, 1762.

OBEDIAH PLATT, administrator of Abigail Trubee's estate."

"Received of David Burr, one of the executors of the last will and testament of Andris Trubee, late of Fairfield; the sum of thirty pounds, lawful money, being in full of the legacy given me in said will.

Fairfield, June 28th, 1760.

EUNICE TRUBEE."

"Received of David Burr, one of the executors of the last will and testament of Andris Trubee, late of Fairfield, deceased; the sum of thirty pounds, two shillings and sixpence, money by a note of hand of Burr of same date herewith, being for a legacy given to Esther Trubee, daughter of said deceased and by his last will.

I say July 1st, 1762, by me as guardian to said Esther.

EZRA WILLIAMS."

"At the Court of Probate of Fairfield, February 10th, 1762, Jonathan Coley, of Fairfield, was by the court appointed guardian to David Trubee, of Fairfield, a minor and the fifth son that hath given bonds."

"At a Court of Probate held in Fairfield, May 5th, 1767; David Trubee a minor of the town of Fairfield, made John Williams of said Fairfield to be his guardian, which the said court accepts, and the said John hath given bond on file as the law directs.

(Test,) A. ROWLAND, Clerk."

Two years after the death of Andris Trubee, his widow became very ill; sorrow and the trials incident to a mother's watchful care over a large family of little ones had proved a burden too heavy to be borne, and Abigail Trubee realized as she lay upon a sick bed in December, 1760, that she would soon be called upon to leave her household band to the care of others. How her heart must have yearned over them. How much need she had of faith and trust as she directed the following will:

"In the name of God, Amen. I, the widow Abigail Trubee, of Fairfield County, and Colony of Connecticut, being in perfect memory, thanks be to God for it, knowing the mortality of my body do make and ordain this my last will and testament, and first I give my soul into the hand of God, that gave it; and as for my body I give it to the earth to be buried at the direction of my executors, and as touching such worldly estate which it has pleased God to bless me with, I will dispose with in this form. And first I will unto all my debts that I owe or shall hereafter owe unto to any person, shall be paid by my executors hereafter named, in a convenient time after my decease.

Item. I will and bequeath unto my youngest daughter the one-half of my estate, unto my youngest daughter Esther.

Item. I will and bequeath the other half of my estate to be equally divided between my other four children, Eunice, Ansel, Alexander and David.

Lastly, I nominate, constitute, and appoint my trusty friend, David Burr, of Fairfield, to be my executor of this my last will and testament; to execute, fullfill, and perform according to the true intent and meaning thereof. In witness whereof I set my hand and seal this 20th day of December, in the year of our Lord Christ, one thousand, 7 hundred and sixty. Signed, sealed, published and pronounced and delivered, the widow Abigail Trubee, as her last will and testament, in presence of

Obediah Platt, Ann Hayes,	Abigail Trubee.
Charles Bennitt.	Seal."

HER WILL PROBATED.

"At a Court of Probate held in Fairfield, March 20th, 1761, personally appeared Obediah Platt, Charles Bennett and Ann Hayes, and made oath that on the 20th day of December, last, they saw and witnessed Abigail Trubee sign and seal, and heard her declare the foregoing instrument to be her last will and testament, and that they then judged her to be of sound mind and memory, and signed and witnessed to the will in her presence. Sworn before the Court.

(Test.)

"At a Court of Probate held in Fairfield, March 17th, 1761, Obediah Platt was by the court appointed administrator of the estate of Abigail Trubee, and hath given bonds on file as the law directs."

I have copied from the inventory taken of Mrs. Andris Trubee's wardrobe such portions as I thought would be interesting for her descendants to read. Her household effects can be found in the Fairfield Records.

INVENTORY.

"1 long coat. 1 silk crape gown. Calmeneo gown and broadcloth coat. Velvet hood and handkerchief. Hood and vail. Holland handkerchief. Sunkikin gown. Great Bible and History Book. Cap and cambric ruffles. Tow cloth. Old Books. Remnant of velvet."

Two children for whom provision was made by Andris Trubee two years previously, are not mentioned in his widow's will—Samuel, aged sixteen years, and Comfort, aged six years. They probably died during the intervening time.

Mrs. Andris Trubee died soon after the writing of her will and was buried with her husband, probably in the yard of their beloved church. Years since the mounds which covered their last resting places were leveled. How few of us knew, as we played in our childhood days upon the Mill Plain green, that beneath our feet, had been laid away amid tears and sorrow, our ancestors whose memory we had been taught to love, respect and cherish.

We have knowledge of but one of Andris Trubee's children. The destruction of the Church Records doomed them to oblivion.

ANSEL TRUBEE.

ANSEL, son of Andris and Abigail Trubee, married Ezebel, daughter of Mr. Joseph and Mrs. Elizabeth Livesley Beers, December 16th, 1769. Mr. Beers was a descendant of James Beers, who came to Fairfield in 1661. He was either a brother or son of Capt. Richard Beers, of Watertown, who was a Pequot soldier. He married Martha, daughter of John Barlow, 1st, and became one of the largest land owners in the town. Mr. Joseph Beers was also a descendant of Lord Bulklaugh, who derived his name from a chain of mountains in Ireland; his family date as far back as King John, of England, in the 12th century.

"The family coat of arms was found in the house of Rev. Gershom Bulkley, D.D., of Weathersfield, Conn., who was a son of the Rev. Peter Bulkley, of Concord, Mass., is thus described : "Argent a chevron between three bull's head cabossed—sable. The motto under it is, "*Nec temere nec timide ;*" "neither rashly nor timidly." This shield with that of Chetwood (the second wife of the Rev. Peter Bulkley), "impaling Chetewode quarterly, orgent and gules, four crosses pattie countersigned, is quite handsome."

"The Rev. Peter Bulkley, son of the Rev. Edward Bulkley, D.D., of the parish of Odell, Berfordshire, England, was born January 31st, 1683, and married, 1st, Jane, daughter of Sir Thomas Allen and, by her, had twelve children. His second wife was Grace, daughter of Sir Richard Chetewode, by whom he had several other children. He came to Massachusetts in 1635, and soon after was regularly installed teacher of the first church of Concord, Mass., (with the Rev. John Jones as pastor), where he died March 9th, 1659, aged 76 years.

"Three of the sons of Rev. Peter Bulkley, viz., Thomas, Daniel and Peter, settled at Fairfield, and from them descend the Bulkleys of the town and county of Fairfield."

At the time of Mr. Ansel Trubee's marriage, the pulse of the American Colonies was beating tumultuously with the feverish throbs of an angry and outraged people preparing to resist the oppressor. Boston was the centre of the movement against unjust taxation. In 1773 occurred her famous "Tea Party." In 1775 the endeavor on the part of the British to arrest two patriots, John Hancock and Samuel Adams, caused the Battle of Lexington. In May, 1775, Dorothy Quincy, the affianced bride of John Hancock, was sent from Boston to Fairfield to remain, while the former place was in danger of destruction. Many other refugees sought the quiet of our village during this political excitement; among them was John Hancock, upon whose head a price had been set, he sought the protection of Samuel Adams, of Fairfield, who was the grandson of our ancestor, Samuel (1st), and consequently cousin of Mrs. Ansel Trubee, and probably a relative of Samuel Adams, of Boston.

For several days John Hancock was not allowed to be seen, but as time passed it was thought safe for him to appear in public. Mr. Adams, therefore, prepared a sumptuous breakfast, to which he invited his neighbours and friends. Just as they were seated around the breakfast board a farmer rushed in crying, "The British! The British! are coming. Can I have the loan of a horse to go after my wife, who is away from home?" For a few moments intense excitement prevailed among the assembled guests as they hastily armed themselves and hastened to the defence of Fairfield. The alarm proved false, but it is said "That breakfast was never eaten by the guests for whom it was prepared."

In 1776 the Declaration of Independence was signed. Fairfield's sons were so active in their efforts to conquer the enemy that the British determined to destroy the town.

On Monday, July 7th, 1779, the sun as it rose over the blue waters of the Sound, cast a radiance over fertile fields and busy homes in the village of Fairfield; a few hours passed, a dense fog had hidden the Sound from view, when the sun suddenly breaking through the mist disclosed the British war vessels anchored off our shores. A Fort on Grover's Hill commanded by Capt. Aaron Turney and Lieut. Isaac Jarvis, (the former was the grandfather of

Mrs. James Staples, of Bridgeport,) made a valiant defence. With only twenty-three men they resisted repeated attacks of the enemy and saved the fort but not the town, for the British troops rushed up the Beach lane a lawless, cruel horde, intent on robbery, and the destruction of the village. Mr. Ansel Trubee's house was situated on the Southport turnpike, and west of the Mill Plain road : his wife was alone in the house with her four little children when she heard the booming of the cannon, and the war cry of the foe; throwing her silver spoons down the well, and a few valuables, she, with a babe in each arm and the other two clinging to her for protection, hastened to Southport. All that day the conflict raged in our village ; men hiding behind trees and fences kept up an incessant firing at the enemy. A few brave women remained in their homes but did not prevent the destruction of their property.

The Bulkley Tavern near the village green, became the headquarters of the British officers. As one of them was coming up the cellar stairs carrying a mug of cider in his hand, a cannon ball struck the house and was imbedded in its walls. "No Yankee fired that shot" he exclaimed. "A Yankee born and bred, for it was fired by none other than brave Captain Aaron Turney," replied his hostess.

That memorable day in Fairfield's history was closed amid the thunder of heaven's artillery, and the incessant flashes of lightning, accompanied by so severe a shower of

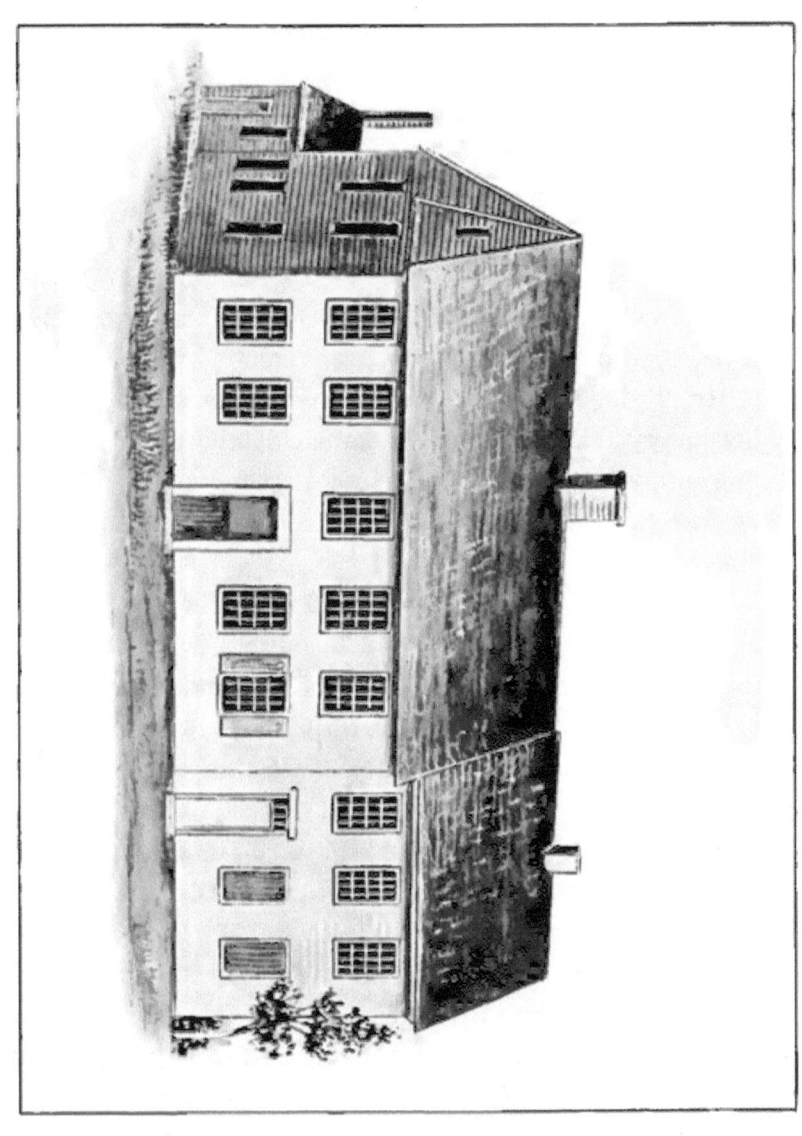

THE BULKLEY TAVERN.

rain as to cause the superstitious to believe the "Day of judgment had come."

As Mr. Trubee and his neighbors gathered around the ashes of their homes, they bravely determined to rebuild and strive to retrieve their losses. That year his name is mentioned in the tax list among the persons who had suffered by the war.

Mr. Trubee possessed a bright and jovial disposition: his happy temperament and musical talent, for he was a fine singer, made him an ever welcome guest. It is said he led the choir in the Episcopal church at Mill Plain many years.

A few years after the war Mr. Trubee bought the property next to the Public School buildings, where he passed the remainder of his life. His farm extended south to the field lane, and north to the terminus of the Rock lot now owned by the heirs of the late Rev. Samuel Osgood, D.D.

Mr. Trubee was successful in his business vocation, which was that of mason and builder, and had contracts for building from Norwalk to Milford. Monday morning he would leave home, on horse back, with empty saddle bags and return home Saturday night with them filled with provisions, but with little gold, for after the Revolutionary war the people were too impoverished to pay in gold and the products of their fields were used instead as a medium of exchange. During Mr. Trubee's absence from home his farm was managed by his growing sons and prudent wife.

Eight children were born to Mr. and Mrs. Trubee, and lived to be men and women, with the exception of William, who was baptized October 14th, 1787, and must have died soon afterward. Their eldest daughter, Abigail, was married by Rev. Andrew Elliott, to Mr. Platt, of Redding. Soon after their marriage they moved west to "the wilderness of the Jerseys." After remaining there a few years they moved to "York State," then in the far west, and all trace of them has been lost.

Eunice, the second daughter possessed a lovely, gentle disposition, a bright and active mind, and a power of adapting herself to both the old and young. She was married, by Rev. Philo Shelton, to Ezra Knapp, who died soon after the birth of their two sons. She then moved to Troy and resided there until her marriage with Joseph White, of Greenfield Hill. Her son Ezra Morehouse Knapp was a speculator in wheat; he invested his fortune of thirty thousand dollars in grain and held it expecting the price would rise, but it fell and Ezra became penniless. Soon after this financial loss he became very ill and hastened to his mother's house on Greenfield Hill, where he died and was buried in the cemetery there, 1834.

Esther, daughter of Mr. Ansel Trubee was beautiful. After her marriage with Mr. Neffis they moved to Troy, N. Y., where they resided until their deaths. They had two daughters, the elder married Mr. Curtiss, of Rochester, and had a large family of children, all of whom are now dead. Mrs. Curtiss was a stately, dignified lady, and her sister Julia, who married Dr. Harral, of New Orleans, brother of Mr. Harral, of Bridgeport, was beautiful. She, her daughter, and her husband have passed away.

Jerusha, daughter of Mr. Ansel Trubee, married Lorenza Craw and moved to another State, and all trace of her was lost.

Sallie, daughter of Mr. Ansel Trubee, married Samuel Staples the great uncle of Mrs. James Staples, of Bridgeport; she survived her husband many years, and died at the old homestead in Fairfield.

On the first day of August, 1814, Ansel Trubee made the following will:

"To whom these presents shall come greeting. Know ye that I, Ansel Trubee, of Fairfield, in the State of Connecticut, being of sound mind and memory, do make and exclaim this my last will and testament. After commending my soul to Almighty God who gave it, I would dispose of what estate it hath pleased Almighty God to bless me with in the following manner, viz.: My just debts and funeral charges being paid by my executors, my will is that my wife Isabel Trubee shall enjoy all of my estate, both real and personal, during the term of her widowhood. And then my will is that my three sons David, Samuel and Andrew, shall come in possession of the same that is not otherwise disposed of in this my will, they paying the following legacies to them, their heirs and assigns forever; to my daughter Eunice, the wife of Ezra Knapp, I give and bequeath twenty-five dollars; to Salley Trubee, one hundred dollars; to Esther, wife of William Neffis, fifty dollars; to Jerusha, wife of Ezra Craw, fifty dollars, to be paid by my sons in eighteen months after they come in possession of the property, and to my daughter Sally, in addition to the above, I give and bequeath my best bed and bedstead together with half the linen which shall be inventoried, and the remainder of my household furniture I would have equally divided among all my daughters, viz., Abigail, Eunice, Sally, Esther and Jerusha, except my clock, to them, their heirs and assignees forever. My will is that David take his portion in the lot on which his house now stands. My will is that Samuel have the barns as a consideration for what I have heretofore done for David, and that Andrew have the house and clock for the same consideration. And I do appoint as executors to this my last will and testament my three sons, David Trubee, Samuel Trubee and Andrew Trubee, and declare all other wills and testaments by me made to be null and void and this to be my last will and testament. Witness I hereunto set my hand and seal this the first day of August, one thousand, eight hundred and fourteen, in presence of the following witnesses, signed, sealed, published, pronounced and declared.

ANSEL TRUBEE.

LUCY SHELTON,
PHILO SHELTON,
HENRIETTA SHELTON."

Mr. Trubee became a communicant of the Episcopal church in 1821. On December 26th, 1823, he suddenly became unconscious and never rallied. He died in the arms of his son Samuel the same day.

HIS WILL PROBATED.

"In Fairfield this 10th day of February, 1824, personally appeared Philo Shelton, Lucy Shelton and Henrietta Shelton, and made oath that they saw Ansel Trubee, the above testator, sign and seal the above written will, and heard him publish and declare the same to be his last will and testament, and that he was of sound, disposing mind and memory, and we all signed the same as witnesses in his presence and in the presence of each other, before me."

AMOS BURR, Jus. Peace.

"At a Court of Probate held at Fairfield, June 30th, 1824, the foregoing will of Ansel Trubee, late of Fairfield, being found is approved and ordered to be recorded.

DAVID MILLS, Judge."

The three sons of Mr. Ansel Trubee, who were executors of his will, met after his death to settle the estate, when Samuel proposed they should set aside the Will in order to divide his father's real and personal property equally with their sisters. To this proposition the brothers agreed and they therefore divided the property equally among all the children.

Mrs. Trubee survived her husband several years, and reached the age of ninety without ever having to wear spectacles, and with her faculties in a normal condition. She had none of the infirmities of old age until a fall caused the breaking of her hip, this shock was, probably, the occasion of her death, which occurred March 16th, 1836.

DAVID TRUBEE.

DAVID TRUBEE.

On March 20th, 1804, David, the fourth child and eldest son of Ansel and Ezebel Trubee, married Charlotte Parrott. His father gave him as a wedding portion his lot north of the main street, upon which he built a pleasant house which is yet standing; here he brought his bride, a beautiful girl still in her teens. The marriage begun so brightly in the spring-time of life and of the season, closed suddenly amidst the snows and ice of mid-winter, 1807.

An infant daughter, whose span of life had been but brief, died a few days before.

In 1808 Mr. Trubee married Martha, daughter of Phineas and Huldah Curtiss, of Stratford, Conn., and sister of the wife of his brother Samuel.

Mr. Trubee possessed a nervous, active temperament, was very witty and fond of relating a good story. When quite a young man he was confirmed in the Episcopal church, but after his second marriage he and his wife became Congregationalists.

Mr. Trubee followed his father's occupation, which was that of master mason and builder. By industry and prudence he acquired a competency. Two daughters were born to Mr. and Mrs. Trubee, Charlotte and Jane Ann. The former remained single; the latter married Mr. Zephaniah Miller, of Fairfield, who with his wife resided with her parents.

Mrs. Trubee, before reaching middle age, became a sufferer from inflammatory rheumatism; this disease caused her hands to become so distorted that they were almost useless, though she could knit, and she usually sat by the sunny south window of her cosy sitting room industriously plying her needles. She was ever patient, and though at times she must have suffered intensely, yet no murmur escaped her lips. Her two daughters lovingly administered to her wants, and when in 1859 her spirit was freed from this earthly bondage they grieved not only for a mother, but also as they who have had taken from their midst a dependent child.

Mr. Trubee lived to be nearly 88 years of age before his summons came.

Mr. and Mrs. Zephaniah Miller had only one child, Arthur Mills. At the age of fifteen he entered a store in New York city; after some years he returned home and entered into business at Bridgeport. After his marriage with Susan, daughter of the late Elihu Sanford, they resided with his parents at Fairfield. About 1875 Mr. Zephaniah Miller built a commodious house on Fairfield avenue, Bridgeport, and moved there the same year.

MRS. DAVID TRUBEE.
(MARTHA CURTISS.)

Arthur Mills and his wife had two children, Arthur and Hattie. Arthur, Sr., was a most devoted son; he always said the relation between himself and father was like the love of two brothers instead of parent and child.

Mr. Miller, his wife, his son Arthur, and Charlotte Trubee, have all passed away.

Mrs. Arthur Mills Miller and her two children, Arthur and Hattie are still residents of Bridgeport.

SAMUEL COMFORT TRUBEE.

SAMUEL COMFORT TRUBEE.

Samuel Comfort, who was the second son of Ansel and Ezabel Trubee, at the early age of four years commenced attending the Mill Plain District School, which was taught by a morose, intemperate old man. Samuel, who was the youngest pupil, became so great a favorite with the teacher that he was honored with the daily task of carrying his jug to a store near the school where it was filled with whiskey. When the morning session commenced the teacher was comparatively good natured, but as the hours passed his temper increased in proportion as the contents of the jug, which was kept by his desk, diminished. When the afternoon session closed he was generally in a semi-stupid condition.

One hundred years ago the village schools were conducted very differently than at the present time; the teacher was generally selected, not for his ability in teaching, but because he was incapacitated for performing physical labor. He was therefore usually uneducated and unfitted for his duties. Many of his pupils were only able to attend school for about six weeks in the winter. At an early age they left school to attend to the duties of the house and farm.

Before vaccination was discovered the law compelled every child to be inoculated, and officers were appointed to go from house to house and take the children who had reached the prescribed age, to the public pest house, where, after receiving inoculation, they were placed in a large room with a number of others who were undergoing the same treatment for prevention of small pox. Their daily food consisted of mush, without salt, as that article was considered injurious for the patient. The fire in the large fire place was not allowed to burn brightly, as heat was supposed to produce fever; if one of the shivering children ventured too near the hearth-stone it was roughly repulsed. Parents were not allowed to remain with their children at the pest-house; they were cared for while there by an incompetent nurse. When the physician pronounced the patient cured it was sent to its parents with the assurance that it would never have small pox.

Samuel Comfort, his brothers and sisters, were obliged to pass through this severe ordeal.

When Samuel was eight years of age the most prominent physician in Fairfield County wished to adopt him as his son, promising that he should have a collegiate and medical education, as he was convinced the bright intellect and pleasing manners of the boy would enable him in the future to stand high in the medical profession. Mr. Ansel

Trubee refused to give his child away, much to Samuel's disappointment, who earnestly yearned for a liberal education, and in after years could never speak of this turning point in his life without expressions of regret.

When Samuel reached the age of eighteen, he had served his apprenticeship with his father. In the autumn of 1805 he determined to visit his sister, Mrs. Neffis, of Troy, and endeavor to obtain work in that city; he was so successful that before mid-winter he had earned a sufficient amount to defray his expenses, and had also saved quite a sum of money. Before returning home in the Spring he visited his sister Abigail, whom he always called Nabbie, and loved very tenderly, as she had taken almost the entire care of him in his infancy: he found her living with her husband and children in a log cabin in the "wilderness of the Jersey's." Samuel received a joyous welcome when Mrs. Platt discovered that the tall young man knocking at her door was the brother who was only a little child when she left her New England home.

That evening as they sat in the light of the bright logs burning in the great fireplace, which almost scorched one's face though shivering from the blasts which blew through the chinks and crevices of the house, stories of each of the dear ones in the family circle were related, bringing the past so vividly before Abigail, that while she listened, the trials of a life in a new settlement was for the time forgotten, and she was a beloved sister and daughter in her girlhood's home again.

After a delightful visit of a few days Samuel was obliged to leave Mr. Platt's, as it was time for the Spring work to commence. The parting between brother and sister was very sad, for they feared years might pass before they met again. He was the bearer of loving messages to the home circle; the last ever sent, for soon afterwards Mr. Platt moved to the "far west in York State," and all trace of Abigail and their children was lost.

Samuel, who had been the leader in all boyish and athletic sports in the village, became, when he reached manhood, the strongest young man in his native town. One day a stranger appeared in Fairfield, who boasted that he was a champion pugilist and boxer, and dared any one to enter into a contest of strength with him. The village youths, proud of Samuel's athletic skill, begged him to accept the challenge. After much persuasion he did so. When the pugilist saw his opponent he treated him with the same haughty disdain as did Goliah the youthful David. Surrounded by a crowd of men and boys the two contestants faced each other; the boxer expecting to knock his adversary out in the first round, advanced in a menacing attitude towards him, when Samuel suddenly rushed forward and clasping his adversary around the waist threw him over his head with such force as to render him unconscious: it was the same feat of strength, so graphically re-

MRS. SAMUEL COMFORT TRUBEE.
(Elizabeth Curtiss.)

lated by Haggard, in the desperate encounter of the young Englishman with the African giant, with this difference, the latter had nearly every bone in his body broken and became a helpless cripple, while Samuel's opponent, when he regained his breath, arose a wiser if not a sadder man, and hastily left the village never to return.

On October 22nd, 1809, Samuel Comfort Trubee and Elizabeth, daughter of Phineas and Huldah Curtiss, of Stratford, were married at Fairfield in the parlor of the house now owned by their granddaughter. She was a beautiful girl, possessing a fair complexion, curly brown hair, blue eyes, and a countenance expressive of great loveliness of character.

Mrs. Trubee was a descendant of William Curtiss, who came with his wife and four children, Thomas, Mary, John and Philip, from England to America in the ship Lyon in 1632. William, the elder son, came the year previous: they settled at Roxbury, Mass. In the records of its old church are recorded William Curtiss and his family; also a description of their "coat-of-arms," which we have given in the genealogical table. The Bearing, dates from the eighth year of Charles I., May 9th, 1632. William (1st) died eight months after his arrival. The family then separated. Widow Elizabeth with William (2nd), and John came to Stratford and settled near their beloved pastor, Rev. Mr. Blackman; the other children remained at Roxbury where some of their descendants are now living.

William (2nd) was well educated: he became prominent in all the public affairs of the town, and was appointed to many important offices: he was also chosen captain of a military organization.

John, though active in promoting the best interests of Stratford, did not take so conspicuous a part as William.

Joseph, the son of John, inherited the sterling qualities of his uncle and became a prominent lawyer. He married Bethiah, daughter of Richard Booth, May 9th, 1676. He became Judge of the County Court, and retained the office many years. He was elected State Senator in 1698, and for twenty-three years retained this office. He was also town clerk until 1727, when he was obliged to resign on account of his advanced age.

His title, "The Most Worshipful Joseph," is still held in honorable esteem by his descendants.

The early life of Richard Booth, father of Mrs. Joseph Curtiss, is shrouded in mystery: it has always been supposed that he was of noble birth, although as far as can be learned he never made that statement.

The ship in which he came to the New World is unknown: it is believed that as England was unwilling to have her nobility leave at that time he, with many others, came under the names of their servants, unfortunately severing their connecting link with the old world.

Richard Booth settled in Stratford, Conn., in 1640. Tradition says that three brothers came from England to

New Haven, Conn. Richard came to Stratford, William settled on Long Island, and the third brother was killed. It seems possible that Richard Booth came first to Boston and settled, as so many of his contemporaries did at that time, at Roxbury, Mass., and came with his neighbors to Stratford. One, Gideon Booth, lived at Roxbury during the early part of the 17th century. He frequently told his grandchildren that he was heir to a vast estate in Wales. This story was forgotten until an agent from England settled in New York in 1850; in his books he had a list of names of parties who had died without known heirs, among them were William Booth, Sir Charles Booth, Sarah Booth, Richard Booth, James Booth, Elizabeth Booth. The will of Charles Booth, late of Hairetsham Place, in County of Kent and Harley street, in the parish of St. Mary's, in the County of Middlesex. Knight, deceased.

The relatives and kindred of said Charles Booth are advised forthwith to send in statements of their several pedigrees, and how and in what manner they made out their relationship and kindred to the said Sir Charles Booth, unto Messrs. Ruddle & Wade, near the Royal Exchange, London, or unto Messrs. J. Ansen & Harpers, Cannon Row, Westminster. Dated 1796, 1803, 1813.

Sir Charles Booth is described as of the middle Temple, London, 1760, Edmond Mapledon of the same place, 1700, John Horsmondon, 1663.

The maternal grandmother of Sir Charles was Ann Mapledon, sister of the above named Edward. Another grandmother's name was Horesmendon.

Nicholas Booth, the last Lord Delemere, was a merchant in London in 1743, and the male issue of Charles' family dying, he succeeded to the title of Lord Delemere. About the year 1670 John Duncan married the daughter of Richard Booth, Esq., alderman of the City of London.

An association was formed by the Booth's in America, to investigate the right to certain English properties. $2,500.00 was raised for that purpose by selling scrip; each scrip was to be $5.00, the holder to be entitled to $300.00 of the money when obtained. Mrs. Dimon, a probable heir to the Booth estate, was selected by the association to go to England with her lawyer, Mr. Knight, and search the records to establish the claim of the descendants of Richard Booth, who was supposed from dates, to have been the son of Richard, son of Sir George Booth, who had married a Massey, of Cheshire. Mrs. Dimon said "The discoveries in her researches that the greater part of the City of Chester belonged to the Booths' in America; that there were valuable estates and many millions in the Bank of England to which they were also heirs." If we had been aware of these facts when we visited Chester how differently we should have gazed upon its ruins, roman walls and ancient cathedral, how faithfully the records of the church and its tombs would have been searched for the name which would have been to us a sesame of untold wealth. Mrs. Dimon, called during her stay in England, upon Thomas Booth, who leased from the crown an estate formerly belonging to Richard Booth, of Chester, the probable ancestor of Richard Booth, of Stratford. He invited her to lunch, and after partaking of wine, the gentleman became very talkative, and informed his visitor where to find recorded the birth of Richard Booth, of Stratford, Conn. Twelve times Mrs. Dimon had crossed the Atlantic in company with her daughter and lawyer to find evidence that Richard Booth, of Stratford, Conn., was the son of Richard Booth, of Massey and Cogshill, Baron in Cheshire, son of Sir William Booth and Elizabeth his wife, daughter of Sir John Warburton. When this startling information was given Mrs. Dimon's passage to America had been engaged, and not wishing to lose her tickets she left the searching of the parish records until a "more convenient season," which never came, as she died while crossing the Atlantic on her thirteenth voyage from New York to Liverpool. No one since then has ever endeavored to search for this wealth.

England's Queen derives the benefit from these Booth estates, as by law they are in ward to the crown until claimed by the legal heirs.

If Richard Booth, of Stratford, had been communicative regarding his English relatives, his descendants in America might now have in their possession ninety millions of England's gold.

Richard Booth, of Stratford, lived to be 82 years of age: he married twice, and had eight children. Some years since a fine monument was erected to his memory in the oldest cemetery in Stratford, and his name appears upon many of the records of the town of Stratford, Conn.

Mrs. Samuel Comfort Trubee's mother was a direct decendant of William Judson, who came from Yorkshire, England, to Concord, Mass., with his family consisting of his wife, Grace, and three sons, Joseph, Jeremiah and Joshua. He settled in Stratford in 1639, and was the first inhabitant of the place. His wife died in New Haven, September 29th, 1659, and he married the widow of Benjamin Mallory. He died in New Haven, July 29th, 1662.

Joshua Judson married Ann, daughter of John Porter, of Windsor, and died in 1661, aged 38 years, leaving a widow and three children, Ann, Joshua and Samuel. Mrs. Judson married for her second husband, John Hurd in 1662.

Samuel, second son of Samuel and Mary Judson, married first Ann Clark, of Milford, December 2nd, 1728. She died and he married Bethea Beach, May 2nd, 1734, by whom he had Abraham, born February 12th, 1735, Ann,

---

NOTE.—Sir William Booth lived at Summerset, where the daughter of Sir William Booth married Mr. Patton, and is buried in the long aisle in the south side of Westminster Abbey. Her mother was Elizabeth, daughter of Sir John Warburton.

THE TRUBEE HOMESTEAD.

born May 12, 1736. Bethea died and he married Abia, her sister, by whom he had a large family, Abia, Samuel, Huldah, who was born October 26th, 1741, Joseph and Hannah. Huldah married (first) Josiah, son of John and Sarah Marchant Gilbert, in 1776. He died and it is said left an infant daughter. His widow married her second husband, Phineas Curtis, son of Joseph (3rd), February 23rd, 1784. They had four children. Hepsibah, married Mr. Barteau; Martha married Mr. David Trubee; Elizabeth married Mr. Samuel Trubee; Huldah married Mr. Jesse Turney. Their son's name is now unknown. Their homestead on Clapboard Hill is gone, but the old well and a few cherry trees still remain.

Soon after Samuel Comfort's marriage, he bought the house in which he and his wife resided until their deaths. He was obliged to have it mortgaged, but by working overhours in a few months he had earned a sufficient amount to pay it off. It was a happy moment in his life when he felt that his home was free from encumbrances and was all his own. In 1810 their first child was born. It was a son and was christened the same year by Rev. Philo Shelton in the old church in Mill Plain, receiving the name of Samuel Curtiss. At this time Mr. and Mrs. Trubee were members of that church. The old Prayer book used by its rector is still preserved and contains a prayer for "Charles I., the Martyr." Mr. Trubee and his wife united with the Congregational church, Fairfield, in 1810, then under the pastorate of Rev. Dr. Hewett, five of their children were baptized by him.

When the day's work was finished Mr. Trubee, taking his infant son in his arms, would walk up and down the path in front of his house, singing to him those good old hymns, which inspired the fathers of old to earnest lives, and noble deeds.

At the time of Ansel Trubee's marriage, America was preparing for the Revolutionary contest. Samuel Comfort's marriage occurred when the United States, wearied with the British outrages to her shipping, determined to resist her barbarities and cruelties. On June 15th, 1812, war was declared which resulted in freeing us forever from England's rule and tyranny. Samuel Comfort joined the militia, when Fairfield was again threatened with destruction from the British; he was one of the soldiers who patroled the beach at night. The gun which he carried during those hours of service is in the possession of Dr. Samuel Garlick. Mr. Trubee was custodian of the company's equipments, and retained them in his possession until our civil war, when the government sent for them

An arcadian simplicity pervaded the home-life of the early New England people. Their cellar was their store, containing a barrel of pork, beef and cider, pails of lard and butter, salted mackerel; flour was ground at the village mill. A pipe and tobacco was always kept by the housewife on a spare shelf for the minister's use when he made his pastoral visit. Divine service was faithfully attended, and although the pews were not luxurious resting places, they were generally filled by an attentive, appreciative people who earnestly listened to the preacher. The open windows of the sanctuary, in the summer, were musical with the buzzing of bees, wasps and hornets, which came sometimes in too close proximity to the worshippers. In winter the edifice was unheated save by the footstoves carried by the ladies. The children and men could watch their breaths upon the frosty air. When, at length, it was decided to have a stove in the church, it was placed upon a high platform to insure the heating of the galleries. The first Sabbath after it had been "set up," two elderly ladies, overcome by "its excessive heat," fainted; when restored to consciousness they were astonished to learn that the stove was cold and fireless.

September, 1825, occurred a gale of terrific force on Long Island Sound; when it ceased the south windows of Mr. Trubee's house were covered with salt, showing that the spray from the Sound had been carried inland for more than a mile.

Six children came to the Trubee household, Samuel Curtiss, William, Elizabeth, Caroline, Harriet and David.

Mr. Trubee's business extended from Norwalk to Stratford; when working at these distant towns he was obliged to leave home early Monday morning, returning Saturday night to find a bright fireside and pleasant tales of helpful, everyday life awaiting him.

One Sabbath morning, in the Summer of 1835, David Trubee, Jr., was sitting during the Sunday-School session by the east window of the church; seeing a sudden flash of light he looked out and saw flames bursting from Knapp's tavern, which was situated on the opposite side of the street. In a moment cries of fire! fire!! resounded from all sides, and people hastened to the scene, where with pails of water they vainly endeavored to quench the flames. When Mr. Samuel Trubee arrived at the tavern he inquired if there was gunpowder in the house; learning that an unopened keg was in the cellar he rushed into the burning building and brought it out in his arms and hastened across the green towards the Academy pond, while sparks from the burning building were falling all around him. Providence preserved his life in an almost miraculous manner, and he succeeded in throwing the keg into the water.

The assembled people cheered until they were hoarse when they witnessed the success of this heroic deed.

In 1837 Mr. Trubee made the following will, and although he lived forty years afterward, it was never changed.

WILL OF SAMUEL COMFORT TRUBEE.

"Know all men by these presents that I, Samuel Trubee, of Fairfield, Town and County, in the State of Connecticut, knowing the uncertainty of life, and while of a sound disposing mind and mem-

GEORGE HOILE.

ory, do make and ordain the following to be my last will and testament, viz.

In the first place I order all my just debts to be paid out of my real and personal estate, as my executors hereafter named may judge to be most beneficial for my estate, and in case they should think it most advisable to apply any part of my real estate for that purpose, they are hereby fully empowered to make sale thereof, and give such conveyances as are necessary to effect that object.

Next. I give and bequeath to my beloved wife Elizabeth, all my household goods and furniture, to be her own forever. I also devise and give to my said wife the use and improvement of the whole of my real and personal estate, so long as she remains my widow, subject, however, to certain conditions and restrictions hereafter named, and in case she should in her judgment stand in need of more than said use and improvement to afford her a comfortable living during the said term of her widowhood, and such of her family as may remain with her during said period, then I authorize my said executors to make her such further advancements out of my estate as the circumstances of herself and family may necessarily require.

Next. The remainder of my estate, both real and personal, I give, devise and bequeath unto my three sons and three daughters, to them and their heirs and assigns forever, to be divided as follows: To each of my sons, who are to share alike, to have one hundred and fifty dollars each more than each of my daughters, and my daughters to share alike, and each to have one hundred and fifty dollars less than each of my said sons, and I further order that so long as any of my children should live with their mother they shall be entitled to a living out of my estate, my sons until they arrive respectively to the age of twenty-one years, and my daughters respectively arrive to the age of twenty-one years, or are married, and in case of marriage of either of my said daughters my estate not to be holden for their support from the time of such marriage respectively; and I further order, in case my daughters should marry, my executors are directed to advance to such married daughter the sum of two hundred dollars each towards their respective portions in my estate, to which payment the legacy and devise to my said wife and not subject, and which sums are to be taken from the whole amount of my said estate except the household goods and furniture heretofore given to my said wife. And I further order that whatever may stand charged on my book against any of my children under my own hand shall be accounted to them respectively as part portion in my said estate.

And I further order, and it is my desire, that in case any of my children should die before my decease, leaving issue, that such issue should be equally entitled to the portion of their deceased parents.

Finally, I do hereby make and constitute my wife Elizabeth, and my two sons Samuel C. and William Trubee, to be the executors of this my last will and testament.

In testimony whereof I have hereunto set my hand and seal this 12th day of August, 1837.

SAMUEL TRUBEE. {L. S.}

Signed, sealed and delivered by testator in presence of Sophia M. Jones, Elizabeth R. Jones, Samuel Rowland.

MRS. GEORGE HOILE.

(Elizabeth Trubee.)

On April 10th, 1837, Elizabeth, eldest daughter of Samuel Comfort Trubee, married, at the age of nineteen, George Hoile. He was the son of Robert Hoile, of Sangate, England. Emigrating to America in his youth, George Hoile, by perseverance and industry, succeeded at his trade and at the time of his marriage was engaged in the carriage manufacturing business in Fairfield. He afterwards removed to Bridgeport and bought a house in the East End. He was a man noted for integrity and uprightness of character; his wife possessed a lovely disposition and was greatly beloved. Never thinking of herself, her life was passed in doing for others; she lived to be more than three score years and ten. Mr. Hoile survived his wife and lived to be 83 years of age. Their daughter, Mrs. Somers, lives in Bridgeport.

Caroline, second daughter of Samuel Comfort and Elizabeth Trubee, married, on October 28th, 1840, Captain Rufus Knapp, son of Captain John and Esther Turney Knapp, of Holland Heights, Fairfield. Capt. John was a descendant of Rodger Knapp, who came with two brothers to this country from England under the command of Winthrop and Saltonstall, in 1630. Rodger settled first in New Haven, and about 1656 came to Fairfield, where he became an influential citizen and large land owner. His descent in England is traced from Rodger de Knapp, who was knighted by Henry VIII., in 1540, for unseating in succession, at a tournament, three horsemen, noted for their bravery and skill. Captain Rufus Knapp's mother, Esther Turney, was a descendant of Benjamin Turney who, it is said, came from Concord, Mass., to Hartford, where he practiced law. About 1642, he came to Fairfield and became one of its largest land owners. His son, Capt. Robert Turney, received many important town offices. Abel Turney, the father of Mrs. Knapp, was a soldier in the Revolutionary war, enlisting in the navy when only sixteen years of age. During an engagement at sea he was shot in the leg and fell. Supposing him dead he was thrown with the slain down the hold of the vessel; after the engagement it was discovered that Abel Turney was only wounded, and he was placed in charge of the ship's surgeon, and recovered, but was always lame. He was granted a pension at the age of 75 years.

When only five years of age, Rufus the eldest son of Capt. John Knapp, arose from his bed one evening, while asleep, and hastily left the house. The family quickly followed the child, but before they could reach him he commenced ascending the tallest tree in the neighborhood whose lowest branches grew twenty feet above the ground; breathlessly his progress was watched as climbing upward he reached the top of the tree, when turning, he quickly descended, and without awaking returned to his bed. This little incident was typical of Rufus Knapp's future life, for he always succeeded in everything he attempted. While yet a boy Rufus asked his father's permission to go on his

CAPTAIN RUFUS KNAPP.

next voyage to sea with him. "It is a dog's life, my son," replied Capt. John Knapp, "I cannot consent to your going." "I shall not disobey you, father," the lad replied, "but when I am twenty-one years of age I shall then go." "If that is your determination you must go now," replied the captain, and though during the trial trip he was obliged to undergo the hardships of a sailor's rough life, he never faltered in his determination to follow the sea. Upon his return home from this voyage, Rufus was sent to the Fairfield Academy to study mathematics and navigation. After finishing this course of study he resumed a seafaring life, and at the age of eighteen years he became captain of a coasting schooner. Soon after he engaged in the southern trade, his trips extending as far south as Florida and New Orleans. After his marriage his bride accompanied him on a voyage to Georgetown, D. C., where at the home of Mr. Dodge she was entertained with true southern hospitality. A few years afterward Rufus Knapp became captain of the ship Leviathan, then the largest sailing vessel plying between New York and Liverpool. From the time he became commander of a vessel Capt. Knapp never met with any disaster but always with success. His sailors were so attached to him that they sailed with him for years. The sailmaker, "Old John," was a most devoted servant, and at odd moments made many little keepsakes for his master's children. The writer has in her possession a box made by him, the cover of which is ornamented with a boat scene where she is represented as seated in the boat clothed in a red coat and green hood. Capt. Knapp had great control over his crew. A passenger for many months upon his vessel, said he never heard him use an ungentlemanly, harsh, or profane word. He was strictly temperate, and never drank wine, even socially, and although he had used tobacco, saying it was " a comfort during a storm," he gave up the habit, claiming it injurious.

A large owner in the vessel he commanded, Capt. Knapp was entrusted by the agents, Sturges & Clermon, of New York, with buying the cargo and shipstores, and his judgment regarding the freights to be carried met with golden returns.

Oftentimes the ship went from New York to New Orleans with freight for the South, where it was reloaded with cotton for the English market. For a few years after his marriage his wife resided with her parents, when Capt. Knapp bought a cottage near Mr. Trubee's to which Mrs. Knapp removed during her husband's absence, and welcomed his return in their own home. Faithfully the wife and mother cared for their home-circle during the long months occupied by him in visiting foreign lands. Six children came to their household. Charles Ansel, the second son, dying in August, 1851, just before his father was expected in port; he reached home in time to attend the funeral. His wife and two of his children accompanied

MRS. RUFUS KNAPP.

(Caroline Truble.)

him upon his next voyage, the trip occupying several months.

Five vessels left the port of New York bound for England November 26th, 1853. Two of them, the Leviathan, of which Capt. Knapp was commander, and the Waterloo were never heard from. The following inscription on a monument erected to Capt. Knapp's memory was composed by his wife.

"We waited, watched, and hoped, but no tidings ever came.
Sad, dark, mysterious thy fate, and hard to bear, yet pleasant remembrances crowd the memory, and like a halo of light, relieve the sadness and best bespeak thy worth."

Mrs. Knapp was a very intellectual woman and possessed both poetical and prose talent. She lived to bring up five children, four of whom are now living at Bridgeport, Conn. Rufus, the eldest son, married the daughter of Mr. Jarratt Morford. They had one child, Maria. Both mother and child died several years since.

On December 6th, 1877, Harriett Trubee, daughter of Capt. Rufus and Caroline Trubee Knapp, was married to Dr. Samuel Garlick. The Garlicks or Gairlochs probably came from the town of that name in Scotland, from which place they crossed to near Leeds, in England, and afterwards, during the wars of the Roses in the middle of the fifteeth century settled upon the mountain in Dinting, near Glossop, Derbyshire, England.

The chapel is still standing upon the hill-top in Charlsworth, where for 700 years the people of Glossop township worshiped. Although the Derbyshire mountains are now nearly destitute of trees, 400 years ago they were said to be covered with a dense forest.

Robin Hood made these woods resound with the musical notes of his bugle. Little John, his lieutenant, was buried in a chapel fifteen miles from Glossop.

Many of the Garlicks, of Dinting, were timber merchants, but in the different wars which were constantly occurring, they were active participants. Several of Dr. Garlick's uncles were in the English army; his uncle Samuel was one of the Coldstream guards at the Tower of London; he was a man of fine presence, and well educated; he was promoted to the rank of captain, and ordered to Gibralter, but died soon afterwards on his way to Spain.

John, the father of Dr. Samuel Garlick, with his wife and four children, left England for America in 1848. During the voyage Mrs. Garlick was taken ill with rapid consumption and died off the Banks of Newfoundland, and was buried at sea. The remainder of the family reached Boston safely, and went immediately to Providence, R. I., where a few weeks later Mr. Garlick died of malignant typhus fever, leaving his little ones to the care of his sister, Mrs. James Middleton. Having no children of her own she endeavored, as far as possible, to fill a mother's place, and brought up this family conscientiously and carefully.

HERBERT MERTON KNAPP.

Samuel, the youngest son, was educated at Westfield; afterwards taught at Kingston, N. Y., New Canaan, and Fairfield, Conn. While at the latter place he commenced the study of medicine with Dr. Dennison. After graduating from Dartmouth he studied nervous diseases at the Lunatic Hospital, Northampton, Mass. He then entered Harvard. After he graduated from that college he practiced medicine for a short time in Shrewsbury, Mass. Receiving an urgent call to Fairfield, he hastened there and immediately entered into practice, remaining until he removed to Bridgeport, where he is now a general practitioner.

He is on the Bridgeport Hospital staff, a member of the Board of Health, a member of the Fairfield County Medical Society, and a member of the Fairfield County Historical and Scientific Societies, etc.

Herbert Merton, youngest child of Rufus and Caroline Knapp, is one of the firm of Burr & Knapp, of Bridgeport, Conn. He was for nineteen years in the employ of the Pequonnock National Bank of Bridgeport, having entered that institution at the age of sixteen years. He held the position of teller during the last ten years of his service. He was one of the original incorporators of the Missouri Trust Company, of Sedalia, Mo., and of the Georgia Loan and Trust Company, of Americus, Ga. He has had the position of vice-president of the last named company since its organization.

Harriet, daughter of Samuel Comfort and Elizabeth Curtiss Trubee, was married July 11th, 1849, to Captain William Knapp, son of Captain John and Esther Knapp, of Holland Heights. As a child, William Knapp displayed an activity and sprightliness which in manhood developed into that determination of purpose which enabled him to succeed in everything which he undertook. When only fifteen years of age he made his first voyage with his brother, Capt. Rufus Knapp. Upon his return from this trip, he attended the Fairfield Academy to pursue the study of mathematics and navigation. After completing these studies he again went to sea with his brother, where he soon rose to the rank of first mate. At the age of nineteen years, he was appointed captain of the schooner Senator, which plyed between New York and the District of Columbia. After a few trips he was given command of the schooner "Dodge," of the same line. During his first voyage he encountered a cyclone, which drove his vessel upon the beach of a Southern coast. At that time there were no life saving stations, with appliances and boats, to rescue the shipwrecked mariner, but as Capt. Knapp stood upon the deck of his vessel, with the waves dashing mountain high, threatening to engulf them, he determined to save both passengers and crew; tying a rope around the waist of one of the seamen who was an expert swimmer, he held it, while the sailor swam towards the shore; how anxiously he was watched as he rose and fell with the

CAPTAIN WILLIAM KNAPP.

rolling of the waves and when at last he was seen on land waving his hand, a shout of rejoicing and prayer of thankfulness was uttered by each person on that shipwrecked vessel. After the sailor had fastened the rope securely Capt. Knapp and his crew, by its aid, carried the ladies safely ashore; among them was an elderly lady—Mrs. Gale, her daughter, Mrs. Professor Gale, her little girl of ten years, and Miss Mary Smith, of Washington, D. C. Completely exhausted and with drenched garments the shipwrecked crew and passengers reached a farm-house where they were given shelter. The vessel soon afterwards went to pieces: the cargo and everything on board was lost. Capt. Knapp, soon after this event, was given command of the brig "Linden," plying between New York and Alabama.

In 1851 he became captain of the brig ship "Aberdeen," plying between New York and San Francisco, and made the quickest trip on record at that time. After several successful voyages, the pilot on entering the Golden Gate, ran the Aberdeen upon the rocks, and although she became a total wreck no lives were lost. In 1853 Capt. Knapp became commander of the clipper ship "Hornet." She was of the Coleman, California Line, noted for her beauty and great speed. In 1856 Capt. Knapp commanded the clipper ship "Cornelia Lawrence" of a European Line. The vessel usually left New York for Alabama, where she reloaded for Liverpool. While the vessel was anchored in the bay of Mobile she was discovered to be on fire; flames enveloped her so completely in a few moments, that the captain and crew barely escaped in the boats, loosing even their clothing. It has always been supposed that the sailors dissatisfied at being obliged to anchor so far from land, caused this conflagration, and as it occurred in the night it had made great headway before it was discovered. In 1857 Capt. Knapp became a member of the New York Marine Society. During the late Civil War, he became commander of the steamer United States, and carried troops South. Capt. Ellsworth and his zouaves went to Louisiana on his vessel. When returning North the shaft of the steamer broke, rendering it helpless and in great danger from privateers. They slowly proceeded by sail until a steamer saw their disabled condition and towed them into port. In 1864 Capt. Knapp superintended the building of the "Guiding Star," and became its commander. This line carried the United States mail. After a few trips he was appointed Port Captain at New York, an office he retained until 1866, when he became captain of the steamship "Evening Star." After a few trips the vessel was caught in a cyclone 180 miles west of Tybee Island, and foundered, with 275 souls on board. Following is the first mate's account of the loss of the Evening Star, published at the time of the disaster:

"We left New York Monday morning with pleasant weather and a prospect of making a quick trip. The next day about four o'clock in the afternoon it blew so hard that we took in sail, and I noticed as the sea rose she worked and strained badly, and I thought of the heavy engine amidships, and the immense freight on board, but having been at sea thirteen years, and feeling so well acquainted with her, felt no uneasiness, though the wind blew a perfect hurricane, a man being scarcely able to stand on deck for it. She soon began to leak and the water came in from all directions. The pumps were set to work, but gave out, and all hands, passengers and crew, men and women, went to work with buckets to try and keep down the water till daylight.

The gale increased and the paddles and wheel-house were carried away during the night. I was sent below to keep the water from coming in at the "dead lights," and had them stuffed with bedding, ladies dresses and everything else we could lay hands on, but every sea that came would turn the ship on her side, and the water would pour in to such an extent that it seemed useless to try to do more. Soon after we were all passing water from the hold in buckets, and several ladies were assisting near me in the line, when the ship gave a terrible lurch, and I thought they would be frightened; but they only quietly asked if we thought the danger great, to which we of course answered in the negative. Those women worked bravely, nobly. A few of the German women gave up in despair, but the American ladies worked on, earnestly and bravely, without faltering, till five o'clock in the morning, when the Captain came down, and told us the vessel must go down.

They had more pluck than many of the men. When the Captain informed all hands that the ship could not hold together long, she was a perfect wreck and floated in the trough of the sea, settling deeper every minute. I was one who went below at this time, to wake up all who were in their staterooms. Several were very sick and did not leave their rooms, going down with the ship. Going on deck soon after I found everybody gathered there, and the wind blew so hard that no human voice could be heard five yards. I assisted in cutting away four boats—we had ten life-boats—the others were also cut adrift. We could not launch them in that sea. Suddenly the ship gave a lurch, and before we knew what had happened, we were under water. It was so sudden I could not realize it. When I came to the surface the water was covered with drift-wood, and I managed to get hold of a plank, which sustained me a short time, and by the little daylight we had, the forms of several passengers and crew could be seen clinging to planks, timbers, boats upside down and anything else which assisted in sustaining them above water.

After being capsized several times, and being badly bruised by the timber floating about, I at last got into the Captain's boat which was supporting eighteen or twenty persons then. A young lady was clinging to her on one side—the only woman I saw alive then out of the eighty or ninety aboard. The boat being full of water was turned over several times by the heavy seas, and we lost our hold on her, but all but one or two regained it. The third time the boat was overturned the young lady lost her hold and sank by my side, almost near enough for me to touch her with my hand, but I could render no assistance.

Captain Knapp soon after lost his hold, when we were capsized, and he went down so near me that I could have touched him if every particle of strength I had, had not at that moment been taxed to the utmost to preserve my hold on the boat. During the twenty-four hours following the sinking of the ship, our boat capsized no less than nine times, the wind blowing a gale all the time."

Statement of Mr. Harris, a passenger.

"Captain Knapp did his duty faithfully and manfully throughout, doing all in his power to save his ship, and when he found there was no hope, contributed much to preserving order among the passengers and crew."

IN MEMORIAM OF CAPTAIN WILLIAM KNAPP.

BY MR. ROBINSON.

"He has gone, a man of noble exterior, warm hearted, of generous impulses, a cheerful companion, a devoted husband, and affectionate parent, a worthy citizen, a faithful officer and a true friend. Though educated to the rough life of a mariner, he ever retained a peculiar gentleness and refinement of manner. Withal he made himself agreeable, and ever took a deep interest in whatever measure was calculated to promote the welfare of his family or neighborhood. He loved, with a sailor's devotion, his home, his native town, and his country. Conscientious in all that he did, his daily walk was that of a Christian gentleman. I, too, mourn him among the dead, for he was my friend. He welcomed me a stranger among strangers, and ever greeted me with a comforting word in the hour of gloom.

Methinks I listen to his voice again, so gentle, and see that smile as genial as a summer's day! But, no, oh captain and friend, thy warfare with the waves and tempest is ended. Thou hast reached that heaven where the storms shall never disturb thee. Sleep on while the ocean chants thy everlasting requiem!"

Mrs. William Knapp and her four children, Isabelle, Elizabeth, Virginia and Lena, continued to reside at her father's after her husband's death. Bravely she met life's duties, and in loving ministrations to her aged parents and little ones, sought by remembering others, to forget herself. Mr. and Mrs. Trubee's old age was made bright and beautiful by the love and tender care of their children and grandchildren. As I write I see again, at eventide, that husband and wife who have passed their sixtieth wedding day; they are seated in their evening room, a large lamp upon a table near them casts a mellow light. Mr. Trubee has a Bible in his hands and is reading its precious promises. Mrs. Trubee, arrayed in a black dress and a cap of spotless whiteness, is knitting. Upon their faces is an expression of rest, contentment, and of peace.

The vision fades.

Those dear old people have received the crown of life. The old home is in a strangers keeping.

Mrs. William Knapp's eldest daughter, Isabelle, on October 31st, 1883, married Mr. George Sanford, son of the late Elihu Sanford. They reside at Bridgeport. On December 8th, 1885, Elizabeth Curtiss married Dr. John Winthrop Wright, son of Mr. and Mrs. Leverett Wright, of Cromwell, Conn. He graduated at Amherst College, and studied medicine at the University of New York City. He is a general practitioner at Bridgeport, Conn., is a

MRS. WILLIAM KNAPP.
(HARRIET TRUBEE.)

member of the Bridgeport Hospital staff, ex-president of the Medical Society, and member of the Scientific Society, etc. Dr. and Mrs. Wright have three children, Bessie, Winthrop and Marion.

On April 6th, 1881, Virginia married Arthur Perry, youngest son of Mr. and Mrs. Curtiss Perry. They reside at Fairfield, Conn., and have five children, Hazel, Maud and Julian. Two boys, twins, died in infancy.

On February 19th, 1889, Lena married Charles Bibbins Bennett, grandson of Deacon Charles Bennett, of Fairfield. They reside with her mother, Mrs. William Knapp, at Bridgeport.

SAMUEL CURTISS TRUBEE.

SAMUEL CURTISS TRUBEE.

SAMUEL CURTISS, eldest son of Samuel Comfort and Elizabeth Trubee, was born August 30th, 1810. When he was fourteen years of age he became a clerk in a store in New York City, where he remained two years. He then returned to Fairfield, where he assisted his father in the mason and building business, until he was twenty-one years of age. A partnership was then formed consisting of Mr. Samuel Comfort Trubee and his two sons, Samuel Curtiss and William.

On January 3rd, 1836, Samuel Curtiss married Clarissa Brown, daughter of Benajah and Sarah Conklin Miller. They resided at Fairfield, where she died February 8th, 1839. Samuel and William Trubee built the original Sterling hotel, and other buildings in Bridgeport and vicinity.

On September 3rd, 1840, Mr. Trubee married Almira Lord, sister of the Rev. Daniel Lord, of Boston. He soon afterward removed to Shelter Island, where he was interested in property. His two children, Samuel Lord, and Almira Lord, were born while they were living on the island. After remaining there four years Mr. Trubee, in

1846, removed his family to Bridgeport, and purchased a house on Lafayette street, where he now resides. His son Samuel Lord died suddenly of croup December 9th, 1848. Almira Lord, his daughter, died March 8th, 1852.

In 1847 he formed a copartnership with Jarrett Morford in the wholesale grocery business. After some years Mr. Trubee retired from active business life. He afterward engaged in the West India trade at Bridgeport with John Hurd, Capt. William Terry, and the new firm of Morford & Trubee. After two years Mr. Trubee retired from mercantile life. At this time he was interested in shipping, and was also engaged in settling estates, and has since been trustee for several estates. For many years he has been a director in the Connecticut National Bank, a trustee of the Bridgeport Savings Bank, and, also, one of its vice-presidents, and is now its president. He has held offices in the Georgia Loan and Trust Company, and other institutions, and has been connected with the Bridgeport and Port Jefferson Steamboat Company, from its commencement, and is now its president. He is also a director of the Bridgeport Hospital.

On January 22d, 1879, Mrs. Trubee died, and on August 14th, 1880, he married Mary, daughter of Isaiah and Caroline Terry, of Wading River, Long Island.

When Mr. Trubee came to Bridgeport to reside it contained only a few thousand inhabitants; he has lived to see it become the second largest city in the State. Ever actively engaged in promoting its best interests Mr. Trubee, both by council and pecuniary aid, has assisted in establishing a number of Bridgeport's most successful mercantile establishments, and is now enjoying good health at the age of 83 years.

WILLIAM TRUBEE.
1865.

WILLIAM TRUBEE.

Sketch of his life by Eliza Ann Trubee, his wife:

"WILLIAM TRUBEE was born May 23rd, 1813. He learned the mason and builders trade with his father and worked with him until he was 21 years of age. He then went into partnership with his father and brother Samuel Curtiss.

On July 30th, 1836, he married Eliza Ann Knapp, daughter of Capt. John Knapp, of Holland Heights, and went to housekeeping in Fairfield, near his father's. He had four sons, William Edgar, Rufus died in infancy, Samuel Curtiss and Frederick. About the year 1840 Mr. Trubee built the Congregational church in New Canaan, Conn. From 1840-46 he spent in building houses in Bridgeport and Southport. In 1847 Bishop & Miller contracted to build the New York & New Haven Railroad, and invited him to superintend the masonry of the road from New York to New Haven, also the depot at New Haven.

In 1850, he with R. B. Mason, engineer-in-chief of the N. Y. & N. H. R. R., with several others engaged on that road, went to Vermont to build the Vermont Valley R. R. from Brattleboro to Bellow's Falls. After this road was completed in 1851, he came home to Fairfield for a short rest. The parties on the Vermont Valley road went direct to Chicago to build the Illinois Central R. R., the first ever built in the west. They wished him to go with them, but he declined on account of the great distance from home. In 1852 he was employed by P. T. Barnum as his agent to attend to his financial affairs at home.

Mr. Barnum resided on Fairfield avenue.

Mr. Trubee built while there a large brick tower, a few rods back of Iranistan, to convey water to the house and grounds. About 1891 this tower was taken down to make room for building purposes, and workmen said it was so thoroughly built that it was easier to break the bricks than the mortar around them. During the three or four years that he was Barnum's agent he filled in the swamp and marsh opposite Iranistan. He laid out State street Extension, which was wider than the other streets in Bridgeport, with the exception of Park and Clinton avenues. Park avenue was then Division street, dividing Bridgeport from Fairfield.

Mr. Barnum and Gen. Noble owned land in East Bridgeport. Mr. Trubee, as Barnum's agent, laid out Washington Park, and several streets and docks, and commenced building up the place, which was then open fields. In 1857 he commenced and largely superintended building the summer residences for New York gentlemen on the banks of the Hudson River.

About 1860 a party of New York gentlemen bought the Evan's place, at Riverdale on the Hudson, and engaged him to superintend the building and laying out of the grounds of several summer residences.

From 1866-70 he was engaged in superintending the building for Legrand Lockwood at Norwalk, Conn. The house cost about $1,000,000, and is sometimes called the Lockwood Palace. It was one of the most elegant residences in the United States.

He superintended the horse railroad in Norwalk until 1874, when he retired from business. On June 9th, 1874, he sold his place in

MRS. WILLIAM TRUBEE.
(Eliza Ann Knapp.)
1894.

Fairfield and moved to Bridgeport, where he built a house on West avenue; it was completed December 20th, of the same year. After removing to Bridgeport he spent the remainder of his life surrounded by his children and grandchildren, who were settled near him. He died in 1881, aged 67 years and 8 months; he was buried in Fairfield, Conn. On his tombstone is engraved the following words written by his sister, Mrs. Caroline Knapp.

'Love such as thine was rare,
The family tie so sacred to his heart, Nothing could sever.
His home, his friends he loved with earnest warmth; but called to part with all he held most dear;
We trust he's found a better home, prepared by one he loved and served so well.'

He united with the Congregational Church in Fairfield early in life.

ELIZA ANN TRUBEE."

William Edgar, son of William and Eliza A. Trubee, married Susan, daughter of Jessop and Susan Alvord, January 10th, 1860.

When only fifteen years of age William Edgar entered his uncle's store, of the firm of Morford & Trubee. Possessing good business talents he eventually became one of the firm and continued in the same until his death, which occurred December 5th, 1890. Four children were born to the Trubee household.

Susie, the eldest daughter, died October 10th, 1865.

Jessie married Henry A. Bishop, the son of ex-president William D. Bishop, of the N. Y., N. H. & H. R. R., and a descendant of Rev. John Bishop, the second minister of Stamford, Conn. Alfred Bishop, grandfather of Henry A., was railroad and canal contractor. The Morris Canal in New Jersey, the great bridge over the Raritan at New Brunswick; the Housatonic, Berkshire, Washington and Saratoga; the Naugatuck and the N. Y., N. H. & H. Railroads were built by him.

Henry A. Bishop is purchasing agent for the N. Y., N. H. & H. R. R., and is paymaster-general, with rank of Brigadier-General on the Governor's staff of Connecticut.

They have two daughters, Margarite and Henrietta. Their first child, a beautiful boy, died in infancy.

Julia A., a daughter of Edgar and Susan Trubee, married Dr. Virgil P. Gibney, of New York City, June 20th, 1893: "He was born near Lexington, Ky., was graduated with the degree of Bachelor of Arts, in 1869, from the College of Arts, Kentucky University, taking afterwards, in 1872, from the same institution, the degree of Master of Arts, and in 1871 from the Bellevue Hospital Medical College in New York, the degree of Doctor of Medicine. Soon after leaving Bellevue, Dr. Gibney was appointed assistant surgeon to the Hospital for the Ruptured and Crippled, and developed so much talent for orthopedic surgery, that he determined to make it his life work. Despite his professional engagements, Dr. Gibney has written numerous articles for journals and encyclopedias, and is author of a standard volume entitled "The Hip and its

WILLIAM EDGAR TRUBEE.

FREDERICK TRUBEE.

Diseases." He is also Professor of Orthopedic Surgery in the New York Polyclinic, one of the two post-graduate medical colleges of the City of New York; is a member of the New York Academy of Medicine, of the State and County Medical Societies, of the Practioners and Pathological Societies, of the American Orthopedic Association, and of the Century, Lotos and Manhattan Clubs."

William Alvord, son of Edgar and Susan Trubee, married Ann J. Rice, daughter of Dr. Rice, of Lockport, N. Y., September 10th, 1890. When almost a boy William Alvord became a clerk in his father's store, where he still remains. They have one child, a son, William Edgar.

Samuel Curtiss, son of William and Eliza Ann Trubee, married Ada Alden, of Westport, Conn. They had two children, Grace and Frank. The former died in 1893. Samuel Trubee has a large apartment house at Buffalo, N. Y. His son Frank resides with him.

Frederick, son of William and Eliza Ann Trubee, married Mary Waterman, daughter of Samuel Baldwin, of Bridgeport, Conn., October 29th, 1868.

When a boy Frederick entered the store of Morford & Trubee as clerk. At the time of his marriage he became a partner of the firm of David Trubee & Co., where he still remains. They have two daughters, Kate and Alice. Kate married Harry Davison, of New York City, April 13th, 1893.

Frederick Trubee has always been an active member of the South Church, Bridgeport, and is a trustee of the Bridgeport Savings Bank.

David Trubee, the youngest child of Samuel Comfort and Elizabeth Curtiss Trubee, was the pet of their household. Inheriting his grandmother's happy disposition, even in childhood he looked upon the bright side of life. When he was fourteen years of age his brothers Samuel and William were engaged in building the Sterling Hotel in Bridgeport. Mr. Sterling, an elderly gentleman and merchant, often watched the young men performing their daily duties, when one day he asked them if they had any brothers at home? "One," they replied, "but he is only a lad." "Is he like you? if so, I wish to see him, bring him to my store to-morrow," said Mr. Sterling. The next morning David Trubee presented himself at the merchant's store and was immediately engaged as clerk. His brothers' good workmanship gained him a position which he filled to the best of his ability. When his brother Samuel became one of the firm of Morford & Trubee, he entered the store as clerk, and soon by his industry and faithfulness became one of the firm, and is now senior partner of the firm of David Trubee & Co. He is also president of the Pequonnock National Bank.

He married Susan, daughter of Elisha and Susan Gifford Doane, December 15th, 1848. They have always resided at Bridgeport, Conn.

DAVID TRUBEE, II.

ANDREW TRUBEE.

ANDREW TRUBEE.

On January 12th, 1823, Andrew, youngest son of Ansel and Ezabel Trubee, married Sarah, daughter of Capt. Aaron Turney, who so bravely defended the fort at Grover's Hill, Fairfield, Conn., during the Revolutionary war. Her mother was a descendant of Thomas Staples, brother of Peter Staples, the ancestor of Mr. James Staples, who, on September 21st, 1858, married Sarah Elizabeth, daughter of Mr. and Mrs. Andrew Trubee of East Bridgeport.

In 1640 three brothers came from England to that part of Massachusetts which is now Kittery, Maine. They were Peter and Thomas Staples, another brother, whose name is unknown, went to Virginia. "Thomas, (Kittery Record says), went west and settled in Fairfield, Conn.," about 1650. He was an active participant in all the public affairs of the town and a large land owner.

In 1650 Goody Bassett for some (now) unknown reason was arraigned in Stratford for witchcraft and was sentenced to be hung. During her trial she said that some persons who held their heads full high in Fairfield were as guilty as herself of this sin. On the way to execution

Goody Bassett was followed by magistrates of the law, ministers of the gospel, and a crowd of the most prominent men and women of the town; as they were passing a large stone by the wayside the condemned woman, overcome with terror, threw herself upon it and clung so tenaciously with her poor manacled hands, that when she was forcibly removed, they were torn and bleeding. Raising them toward heaven she prayed that if she was innocent the print of her bleeding hands might appear upon the stone. It is said the following morning they did appear, and remained until a few years since, when an unbeliever removed the stone to build a cellar wall.

Remembering her words regarding the witches of Fairfield the people of that village commenced searching for suspicious characters. Goody Knapp was selected as a victim of the popular superstition of the times; Mr. Thomas Staples, and his wife, by speech and action endeavored to save her life. It was a dangerous thing for them to do, as it was believed the witches defended their friends. By persuasion and council the minister of the Congregational church and its people endeavored to elicit the statement from Goody Knapp that Goodwife Staples was an accomplice. " You would have me say," she said to her tormentors, " that Goodwife Staples is a witch, but I have enough sins of my own to answer for already, and I hope I shall not add to my condemnation—I know nothing against Goodwife Staples." Notwithstanding her unpopularity

MRS. ANDREW TRUBEE.

(Sarah Turney.)

Mrs. Staples continued to intercede for Goody Knapp's life, protesting that she doubted there was such a thing as witchcraft. Her efforts were fruitless, and one beautiful morning Goody Knapp was led to the hill, opposite what is now Dr. Warner's property in Fairfield, to suffer death by hanging. After ascending the ladder she requested to be taken down as she had something to say. As she approached her pastor, he said, "Is Goodwife Staples your accomplice?" "All I know," she said, "is that one morning two Indians came to her house with two little images that were bright and shining, and begged her to buy them, saying that by rubbing them every wish would be granted." "Did she buy?" was asked. "I know not," was answered. "You may lead her back" said the minister. As she lay upon the ground after death the women gathered around her to find the witch marks. Kneeling by the prostrate form, Mrs. Staples, wringing her hands in agony, raised them heavenward, while tears streamed down her cheeks cried, "Lord, lay not this charge upon us and our children." Rodger Ludlow, and others, deeming Mrs. Staples guilty, repeated this story and said undoubtedly she was a witch; whereupon Mr. Staples instituted suit against them for defamation of character, and so strongly and vigorously was it prosecuted that witchcraft was stamped out in Fairfield; probably saving the town from the terrible scenes which were enacted in Salem, Mass., during its witchcraft mania of 1692.

Mr. Andrew Trubee, after his marriage resided in Bridgeport, where he successfully pursued the business of mason and builder. His contracts extended as far as Milford. He built the first three brick buildings in Bridgeport. They are still standing on Wall street.

Inheriting the lovely disposition of his mother, he was beloved by all both young and old. Mrs. Trubee possessed a ready wit and an ability which enabled her to be a wise counselor and a most excellent housekeeper. Two children came to their household, Sarah Elizabeth and Francis Louise. The latter died Sept. 17th, 1849. Mrs. Trubee died Dec. 8th, 1868.

Mr. Trubee survived his wife, and died Nov. 11th, 1875, mourned by his immediate circle of relatives and friends.

JAMES STAPLES.

JAMES STAPLES.

When a child of seven years of age, James Staples was one day running after a horse which had been left untied, by its owner, intending to fasten it to a post, when it turned viciously and threw him down; rearing it struck the prostrate boy and broke one arm in several places and badly bruised his side. With rare presence of mind the little fellow pretended he was dead: the horse carefully watching him commenced walking towards the road. When the child thought him far enough away to allow his escape, he arose and started for his house a few rods distant. With a squeal of rage at the escape of his victim, the horse pursued the child. Crying for help, James reached the house, and rushed into his sister's arms, who was in the open door-way looking for the cause of the screams. The animal was running so swiftly he was hardly able to check his speed in time to save himself from striking the building.

That spirit of bravery and fortitude has been a characteristic of Mr. Staples' life.

James Staples' childhood was passed upon his father's farm at Swanville, Maine, with his eleven brothers and sisters. They not only made the house ring with mirth and laughter, but aided their mother in the management of the house and farm while their father, who was a sea captain, was absent from home. At the age of seventeen, James was prepared for college, but was unable to enter on account of ill health caused by too close application to study. After this great disappointment he accepted a position as teacher, and meeting with success, followed the profession until 1852; when repeated trials caused him to resign and leave his native town. In that year his brother, Hezekiah, captain of the brig "J. W. Godfrey," was lost while coming from Florida to Maine. Richard, another brother and passenger on this vessel was also lost. His brother Josiah, captain of the brig "Mariel" was lost on Cohassett Ledge, April 6th, 1852. Samuel, a brother, died at the West Indies, Oct. 7th, 1852, and a brother-in-law died this same year, also his wife and an only child. On Sept. 21st, 1858, he married Sarah Elizabeth, daughter of Mr. and Mrs. Andrew Trubee of East Bridgeport, Conn.

In 1854 Mr. James Staples came to Bridgeport where he engaged in the lumber business, and met with success until the crash of 1857, when through the failure of other firms, he lost a fortune. Mr. Staples was not disheartened by this financial disaster, but with the perseverance inherited from his ancestress, Sarah Trefethern Staples, he soon retrieved his losses, and at the present time is senior partner of the banking firm of "James Staples & Co."

MRS. JAMES STAPLES.
(SARAH ELIZABETH TRUBEE.)

He is an active member of the Board of Trade, and has been instrumental in establishing many large manufacturing interests in Bridgeport, is also an ex-member of the Board of Education, and is president of The Consolidated Rolling Stock Co.

His son Frank Staples, a partner of "James Staples & Co.," married Laura Francis, daughter of Mr. and Mrs. William Stevens, Dec. 16th, 1884. They have one child, Richard Trubee, born Sept. 4th, 1885.

This history of the Trubee Family is completed.

May the blessing given to our fathers, and inherited by us, descend upon our children unto the third and fourth generation, and through them unto all time.

END.

LOYAL AU MORT.

Adams.

ADAMS.

"The family of Adams (meaning red-adamah—red-earth,) can claim the distinction of being the oldest individual name on record. The surnames of modern times are said to have originated during the Crusades of Palestine; the baptismal name alone having been before that time in common use among Christians. The Chieftains in the crusading expeditions then assumed the names of the places whence they came, or of the estates of which they were owners. The common soldiers added the christian names and hence the surnames of christian names with the addition of 'son' thus Adams' son became Adamson, in the Scotch, MacAdam. The artisans assumed the names of their trades, which passed to their children and descended to their posterity."

"The earliest record of the English branch of the Adams family is that of John app. Adams of Carlton Adams, in Summitshire, who married Elizabeth, daughter and heiress to John Lord Gourney of Beviston and Tindenham, County of Glouster, who was summoned to Parliament as Baron of the Realm, 1296 to 1307."

"In the upper part of a Gothic window on the southeast side of Tindenham church near Chopston, the name of John app. Adams, 1310 and 'arms argent on a cross gules five mullets or' of Lord app. Adams are still to be found beautifully executed in stained glass of great thickness and in perfect preservation."

"This church is still in a good state of preservation. It originally stood with the boundary of Wales, but at a later period the boundary line was changed and it now stands on English soil. The Arms and Crest borne by the family is,

> Arms: *Argent on a cross gules, five mullets or,*
> Crest: *Cut of a ducal coronet a demi-lion.*
> Motto; *Loyal au Mort.*

"A motto commonly used by this family is 'Aspire, Persevere and Indulge not,' still another '*Sub Cruce Veritas*'."

"App Adam (1) came out of the Marshes of Wales (Lords of the Marshes were noblemen who in the early ages inhabited and secured the Marshes of Wales and Scotland, ruling as if they were petty kings with their private laws.) These were subsequently abolished."

Copied from History of Adams Family by Henry Whitmore.

GENEALOGY OF THE ADAMS FAMILY OF FAIRFIELD, CONN.

Edward Adams was at New Haven in 1630. At Milford in 1646 and at Fairfield in 1650. His wife's name was Mary. He probably died 1671.

THEIR CHILDREN.

Samuel, Abraham, Mary, who married (1st) Luke Guire, (2nd) Mr. Merwin.

Nathaniel, John and Nathan.

Nathaniel and John died unmarried.

Samuel Adams, son of Edward and Mary Adams, by first marriage had Samuel, born Jan. 1st 1677, Daniel, born May 17th, 1679.

He next married Mary, daughter of Robert Meeker, July 15th 1679.

ADAMS.

THEIR CHILDREN.

Sarah, born Oct. 3rd, 1680, married Isaac Castle of Woodbury. Abagail, born Mar. 25th, 1682, married Elijah Crane of Stratfield. Elizabeth, born Feb. 3rd, 1684, baptized and covenanted Apl. 29th 1705. Abraham, born Jan. 1st, 1685. Jonathan, born Oct. 1686. David, born June 24th, 1689. Benjamine, born Dec. 28th, 1690. John, born Sep. 6th, 1692.

Abraham Adams, son of Edward and Mary Adams was baptized Dec. 9th, 1694, and entered into full communion the same day. His wife's name was Sarah.

THEIR CHILDREN.

Deborah and Hannah baptized June 20th, 1694. Mary, Abagail, Susanna and Elizabeth, baptized Feb. 24th, 1695.

Abraham, died in 1728 and was buried in the churchyard at Mill Plain where it is supposed all the Adams family are interred. The church on the Plain was burned and all the records consumed with it. We have thus lost the church history of the Adams family who were Episcopalians.

When the church yard was made into a park the cemetery was destroyed, a few stones were removed to the old Fairfield cemetery, among them Abraham Adams'.

Nathan Adams, son of Edward and Mary Adams, with his wife Mary, covenanted Dec. 9th, 1694.

THEIR CHILDREN.

Nathan, baptized Oct. 11th, 1696. Nathan, baptized Oct. 2nd, 1698. Nathan, baptized Sep. 12th, 1700. Avis, baptized Nov. 29th, 1702. Nathaniel, baptized Oct. 1st, 1704.

Abraham Adams, son of Samuel Adams, died and his property was divided Mar. 8th, 1720. His wife's name was Sarah. He owned Horden's Hill, which lies west of Moody's Mill, Bridgeport. Sarah, widow of Abraham, covenanted Mar. 30th, 1720.

Samuel Adams lived at Barlow's Plains. His church record was probably destroyed in the Mill Plain Episcopal church when it was burned.

Jonathan Adams, son of Samuel, (1st) married Mary, daughter of Samuel and Edere Couch.

David Adams, son of Sam'l (1st) married Abigail ———. Their daughter Annie, was baptized Feb. 12th, 1716. David, their son, was baptized Feb. 8th, 1719, and entered into full communion July 5th, 1741.

Daniel Adams, son of Sam'l (1st) married Rebecca ———. Their children Rebecca, baptized Aug. 30th, 1702, married Joshua Jennings, Feb. 3rd, 1726. Samuel, baptized Mar. 19th, 1703. Daniel, baptized June 29th, 1707. Sarah, baptized 1711. Elizabeth, baptized June 2nd, 1717.

BISHOP.

Alfred Bishop married Mary Ferris.

THEIR CHILDREN.

Ferris, William Darius, Henry.

William, son of Alfred and Mary Ferris Bishop, married Julia Ann, daughter of Russell and Maria Hitchcock Tomlinson of Bridgeport.

THEIR CHILDREN.

Russell, Henry, William, Mary.

On February 6th, 1883, Henry Alfred, son of William and Julia Ann Bishop, married Jessie, daughter of William Edgar and Susan Curtis Trubee of Bridgeport.

THEIR CHILDREN.

William Alfred, born July 25th, 1885; died August 24th, 1886.
Marguerite Alvord, born August 29th, 1887.
Henrietta, born Nov. 18th, 1893.

BEERS.

GENEALOGY OF THE BEERS FAMILY.

James Beers first settled at Southport; he was deeded by the Indians eight acres of land where the Congregational Church now stands; he also had 18 acres of land confirmed to him by the town of Fairfield on the west side of Sasco River, Feb. 10th, 1661. It is said that he was a son or brother of Captain Richard Beers, a Pequot soldier, in Watertown. He became one of the largest land owners in Fairfield. He married Martha, daughter of John Barlow, 1st, by whom he had several children. His will is dated Mar. 14th, 1694, and he probably died soon afterward.

CHILDREN.

Joseph (1st).
Martha, wife of Joseph Bulkley.
Deborah, wife of Samuel Hull.
Elizabeth, wife of John Darling.
James.

James (2nd), married a daughter of Captain Richard Osbon and lived for a while at Pequonnock, then at Woodbury, but removed to Fairfield and purchased land at Saco hill.

CHILDREN.

Sarah, born May 8th, 1673.
James, June 28th, 1677.
Joseph, July 11th, 1679.
David and Mary.

He died leaving a large estate.

Joseph (1st), son of James Beers married Abigail, daughter of ——

CHILDREN.

Joseph, born March 13th, 1689.
Abigail, April 24th, 1692.
James and probably others.

He died 1692 leaving a good estate.

Joseph (2nd) and Hannah Whitlock were married March 1st, 1711.

CHILDREN.

Joseph, born Dec. 19th, 1711.
Sarah, born Nov. 12th, 1714.
David, born April 27th, 1717.
Abigail, born Oct. 11th, 1721.

David married daughter of James Livesey.

Joseph Beers, Jr. (3rd), married Elizabeth, daughter of James Livesey, Sept. 21st, 1738.

CHILDREN.

Reuben, born Nov. 21st, 1739.
Sarah, born Sept. 19th, 1743.
Isabel, born July 14th, 1745, married Ansel Trubee, of Fairfield Dec. 15th, 1769.
Abigail, April 24th, 1747.
Elizabeth, April 28th, 1752.
Joseph, May 28th, 1754.
Abigail died Sept. 13th, 1815, aged 68 years.

BENNETT.

Charles Bibbins Bennett, grandson of Deacon Charles Bennett of Fairfield, married Lena Knapp, daughter of William and Harriet Trubee Knapp, Feb. 19th, 1889.

BEACH.

John Beach appears first in Stratford Records in 1661. He had eleven children.

Joseph, the 10th child, born Feb. 5th, 1671, married Abiah, daughter of Ebenezer Booth, before 1697. They had seven children.

Berthia married Samuel Judson in 1734.
Abiah married Samuel Judson as second wife 1737.
Joseph Beach died Dec. 17th, 1737.

BOOTH.

Description of the Booth Coat of Arms—

   Crest: a lion passant, ar

   Shield: ar three boars heads, erect, erosed, sable, langued, gulse.

   Motto: Quod ero spero (What I shall be I hope.)

Booth, originally Barton, Co. Lancaster and subsequently of Durham Massy Co., Chester, decended from William de Booth living in 1279, son of Adam de Booth. Sir George Booth 2nd, last of Durham Massy was created Baron Delemere in 1661, and his son Henry 2nd Lord Delamere made Earl of Warrington, left an only daughter and heir, Lady Mary Booth, married to Henry Grey 4th Earl of Stamford. At decease of George 2nd Earl of Warrington, the Barony of Delemere passed to his cousin, Nathaniel Booth as 6th Lord. He died without surviving issue, leaving his two sisters his co-heirs.

Elizabeth married to Charlton Thrupp, Esq., and Vere who married George Tyndale Booth, Tyndale, of Hoyling, Eng.

GENEALOGY OF THE BOOTHS IN ENGLAND.

The following matter is an abstract from Kimber & Johnson's Baronage Vol. I, London, 1771, and Nicolas' Peerage Vol. I, 1825.

"This family name which can still be traced back six hundred years, first occurs in the county Palatine of Lancaster, where a son of

Booth

Adam DeBooth was living in 1275. All the other families of this name in various parts of England are believed to be derived from this parent stock through its younger branches. The spelling of the name has been various. Some of the names given are Both, Bothe, Bouth, Bouthe, Boothe, Booth."

"The principal documents relating to the early history of the family were, (in 1771,) in possession of the Countess Dowager of Stamford, and of George Booth of Tyndale, Esq., lineal descendants of the principal house," Lancaster county, 1275.

"William, (son of Adam) de Booth, married Sybil, daughter of Ralph de Brereton of the county Palatine of Chester. The Brereton's were an ancient family dwelling at Brereton in that county. The male line or its title became extinct at the death of Francis, Lord Brereton, 1721.

"Thomas de Booth, son and heir of William had issue ; John, or (as better authority of a deed says) 'Robert who was living in the time of Edward II, from 1307 to 1327. Robert (or John) Booth married in the Barton family of Lancashire, but evidence is not clear whether his wife was Agnes, daughter and heir of Sir William De Barton, or her daughter and heir, Loretta. The latter seems more probable. He had a son and heir, Thomas, of Barton, knight, (styled Thomalin of the Booths). He was living in the time of Edward III. (1327-77.)"

His seal (as appears by an ancient document in possession of Lord Delamere in 1680) was, (in 1372) a chevron engrailed in a canton, a mullet; and for crest, a fox and a St. Catherine wheel with the motto, '*Sigillum Thoma.*' He married Ellen, daughter of Thomas De Workesly (now Worsley), near Booths, Lancashire.

By her he had three sons and four daughters, John, Henry, Thomas, Alice, Catherine, Margaret, Anne.

John, son and heir of Sir Thomas, was living in the time of Richard II., and Henry IV. (1377 to 1413). He is styled John of Barton, and bore as his paternal arms, the ancient Booth device, viz., three boars heads to which from his Barton estate he added another, viz., argent a fesse gules by the name of Barton.

He married (1st) Joan, daughter of Sir Henry Trafford, of Trafford, in Lancashire, knight. The Traffords were of very ancient name, and dwelt in Lancashire before the time of William the Conquerer. After her death he married Maude, daughter of Sir Clifton Savage, of Clifton, in Cheshire, knight. The children of Sir John Booth, and Joan, his wife, were seven sons and five daughters, viz., Thomas, Robert, William, who became Bishop of Litchfield and Coventry 1447, and Archbishop of York 1452. Richard, Roger, John, Ralph, Margery, Joan, Catherine, Alice, Lucy.

The issue of Sir John Booth and his wife Maude, was Laurence; was made Bishop of Durham 1457, Archbishop of York 1476. He was also keeper of the Privy Seal 1457, under Henry VI., and 1474 under Edward IV., was Lord High Chancellor of England. He died 1480.

Thomas Booth, son and heir of Sir John, was knighted in the fourteenth year of Henry VI. (1436). He married a widow Weaver, who was daughter of Sir George Carrington, knight. By her he had four sons and three daughters.

Thomas married Anne, daughter of Sir John Ashton, and had issue, but it failed in the next generation. John was killed at Flodden Field, 1533. Henry died unmarried, Nicholas died unmarried. Margaret, Anne, Dorothy.

By reason of the failure of the male line in Thomas Booth's family, that of his brother Robert became the head branch, and has so continued. (Richard Booth's probable ancestor.) Robert was the first of the Booths who settled at Dunham Massey, in Cheshire. He died Sept., 1450, and is buried in the Parish church of Wilmerton in Cheshire. He married Dulcis, daughter and heir of Sir William Venables, of Bollen, knight. She died Sept., 1453.

Sir Robert Booth, and William his son, had a grant of the sheriffalty of Cheshire for both their lives and the survivor of them. Sir Robert Booth and his wife Dulcis had a numerous family, nine sons and five daughters. William, Ralph, Geoffrey, Hammond, LL.D., John, LL.D., was made Bishop of Exeter, 1465; died 1478. Edmond, Peter, Philip, Lucy, Ellen, Joan, Alice, Margaret. Robert was Dean of York; died 1487.

Sir William, eldest son and heir of Sir Robert Booth, of Dunham Massy, knight, married Maude, daughter of J. Dutton, Esq., of Dutton in Cheshire. She survived him and married again. By her he had five sons and nine daughters. He died April, 1478.

Sir William Booth received of Henry VI. an annuity for service to the crown. His children, George, Richard, Laurence, John, William, Dowse (probably nickname for Dulcis), Anne, Ellen, Margery, Alice, Elizabeth, Joan, Isabella, Catherine.

Sir George Booth married Catherine, daughter and heir of R. Mountfort, of Bescote, in county of Stafford. The Mountforts were of noble connection, being related to David, King of Scotland, and to the great family of Clinton.

This marriage brought to Sir George Booth an ample estate of manors and lands in the counties of Salop, Stafford, Warwick, Leister, Hereford, Wilts, Somerset, Devon and Cornwall.

By his wife Catherine he had three sons and two daughters. He died 1483, (first year of Richard III.) His children, William, Laurence, Roger, Alice, Ellen.

Sir William Bothe, of Dunham, Massey, knight, was twice married, first to Margaret, daughter and co-heir of Thomas Ashton, knight, by his wife Anne, daughter of Lord Greyslock and Wemm, by whom a large inheritance in Lancashire and Cheshire came to the family of Booths.

This property in 1771 was in possession of the Countess Dowager of Stamford. Mrs. Margaret Booth, wife of Sir William, died before 1504. He then married Ellen, daughter and co-heir of Sir John Montgomery, of Kewby, in Staffordshire. By his wife, Margaret, he had children, George, John. By his wife, Ellen, he had William, Hammet, Edward, Henry, Andrew, Jane, Dorothy, Anne. Sir William Booth possessed various manors in Cheshire, Yorkshire, and Cornwall. He died November 19th, 1519, and was buried in Bowden.

George Booth, Esq., son and heir of Sir William, married Elizabeth Butler, of Beausay, near Warrington in Lancashire whose progenitors had been summoned to Parliament in the reigns of Edward I. and II. By her he had four sons and seven daughters. He died 1531, aged 40 years. (22nd year of Henry VIII.) Children: George, John, Robert, Roger, Ellen, Anne, Margaret, Elizabeth, Dorothy, Alice, and Cecil.

George Bothe, eldest son and heir of Sir George, was born 1515 or 1516, and died 1544, aged 28 years. He married in 1531, when only sixteen years of age, Margaret, daughter of Rowland Bulkley, of Benmorris (Anglesea). By her he had no issue. After her death he married Elizabeth, daughter of Sir Edmond Trafford in

Lancashire, knight. To him as one of the titled families of rank came an official letter, Oct. 12th, 1529, announcing by command of Queen Jane Seymour, the birth of her son, afterward Edward VI. It is dated on the day of his birth. This letter was preserved by Mary, Countess Dowager of Stamford 1771, as was also another from Henry VIII. to Sir George Bothe, Feb. 10th, 1543, concerning forces to be raised against the Scots. Elizabeth, wife of Sir George Bothe died in 1582. Both of them lie buried at Trentham church, Staffordshire. By her, the mother of his children, he had William, 1541, Elizabeth, Mary, Anne.

William Bothe, son of Sir George, was but three years old when his father died, and therefore, was in ward to the king.

He married Elizabeth, daughter of Sir John Warburton, (of Airley in Cheshire), knight. He became sheriff of Chester, 1571, and was knighted 1578, and died Sept., 1579, in his 39th year. He was buried at Bowden. His wife died Dec. 1628.

They had seven sons and six daughters. William; died before his father. George, born 1567. Edmund; a lawyer—died without issue. John died 1644, leaving three sons and one daughter. Robert, an officer in the army—died 1628. Peter died young.

Richard married a Massie of Cogshill, in Cheshire, and died 1628. From him the Booths, of Barrow, in Cheshire, are descended. Eleanor, Susan, Alice, Dorothy, Elizabeth, Mary. This Richard is supposed to have been the father of Richard Booth, of Stratford.

Sir George Bouthe was by reason of his minority in ward to the crown.

Queen Elizabeth, thereupon, granted the use of his estates to her favorite, Dudley, Earl of Leicester, to the great detriment and expense of Sir George in afterward obtaining possession of his lands.

He was of age in 1587, and knighted near the end of Elizabeth's reign, and was created a Baronet by patent, under James I., 1611. Sir George Bouthe had two wives. First, Jane, daughter and heir of John Carrington, of Carrington, 1577. By her he had no issue. His second wife was Catherine, daughter of Sir E. Anderson, Chief Justice of the Common Pleas. By her he had five sons and seven daughters. He was twice high sheriff of Cheshire, and as often of Lancaster. He died in 1652, aged 86 years. His children: William, Francis, born 1603, died 1616, Thomas, born 1604, died 1632. Edmund, born 1608, died 1617, John was knighted by Charles II. His second son, John, had a son Thomas who died unmarried in America in 1700. Mary, Catherine, Elizabeth born 1616. Four names are not given.

William Bouthe, Esq., eldest son of Sir George married Vere, second daughter of Sir Thomas Egerton, eldest son of Lord Chancelor Egerton, Viscount, Brakesly. By her he had five sons and two daughters. He was Knight of the Shire of Cheshire and 'Custus rotulorum' for Cheshire by commission. This office remained in the family with short intermission till 1693. He died before his father, Sir George, April, 1636, so that his son the grandson of Sir George was in his stead successor to the Baronetcy.

The children of William Bouthe, Esq., and Vere his wife, were Thomas; born 1620, died 1632. George; born 1622. William; died young. Nathaniel; grandfather of Sir George Booth, who was living in 1771. Charles; died young. Elizabeth; died young. Catherine; born 1624, died 1667. Sir George Bouthe (117), second son of the above William, was born 1622, and died 1684. At his father's death he became ward to the crown. He was subsequently member of Parliament for the county Palatine of Chester, commander-in-chief of his majesties forces in Cheshire, Lancashire, and North Wales, and, after the Restoration, was for eminent services created, by Charles II., Baron Delamere, of Dunham Massey ; but at length, not being obsequious enough to that corrupt king, was neglected by him, and ill used by his successor, James II.

George Bouthe, first Lord Delamere, married, 1st, Catherine, daughter and heir of the Earl of Lincoln. She died at the birth of her first child, 1643. He then married Elizabeth, eldest daughter of Henry Grey, Earl of Stamford who died 1690, having had seven sons and six daughters. The children of Sir George Bouthe, a daughter, Vere, by his first wife Catherine, born 1643 died unmarried 1717. She had right to the Barony of Clinton. By his second, wife, Elizabeth, he had, William ; born 1648, died unmarried, 1661. Henry. Charles ; died unmarried. George. Robert ; born 1666, died 1730; married Anne, daughter of Sir Robert Booth, of Salford, and had issue, of whom Nathaniel, born 1709, died 1770, succeeded his first cousin as Baron Delamere. The Barony expired with him. Cecil. Neville. Elizabeth, born 1645; married Edward, Earl of Conway. Anne; died young. Jane; died young. Diana. Sophia; died very young.

Henry Booth (125) second Lord Delamere and second son of Sir George, succeeded to the Peerage on the death of his father, 1684. His eldest brother William having previously died. He was Knight of the Shire ' Custos rotulorum' and member of several Parliaments. He favored the Bill of Exclusion guarding the Protestant succession for which he was thanked by Lord Russell on the morning of that nobleman's execution. In the latter years of Charles II , and after the accession of James II., he was twice committed to the Tower and at length tried under the last named tyrant for high treason and unanimously acquitted by a Court of twenty-seven Peers.

Afterward he retired to Dunham, Massey, until the Revolution, when he was one of a committee of three Noblemen appointed by the Prince of Orange to demand of James that he remove from Whitehall. He was made Privy Councellor, Chancellor of the Exchequer and in 1687 Earl of Warrington. He died 1693. His wife's name is not given.

HENRY BOOTH'S CHILDREN.

James died in infancy. George, born 1675, Langham, born 1684, Henry, born 1687, died 1727, Elizabeth, died 1697, Mary, died 1742.

George Booth, second Earl of Warrington, married in 1702, Mary, daughter of John Redburney, of London, and by her he had Mary, born 1703. Upon the death of the Earl Aug. 2nd, 1758 without male offspring, the Earldom became extinct. It was, however, as we shall find revived in the line of Harry Grey, Earl of Stamford, who married Mary Booth (143), daughter of the last Earl of Warrington. Meantime the Barony of Delamere descended to Nathaniel Booth, who was the second son of Robert, and own cousin to George the last incumbent. Nathaniel Booth died in 1770, without male offspring, when (according to Nicolas' Peerage Vol. I. p. 191) the Barony became extinct.

But according to Kimber and Johnson's Baronage, Vol. I, the title passed to George Booth, son and heir of John, who was son of Nathaniel, who was fourth son of William.

This George, Baron Delamere 1771, was then second cousin to George, the last preceeding Baron and Earl, and cousin to Nathaniel the last Baron. But with this George the son of John who seems to have had only two daughters the title expired.

From Nicolas' Peerage (Vol. I, p. 181), we learn that in April, 1796, George Harry Grey, fifth Earl of Stamford, and son of Harry Grey, fourth Earl of Stamford, by Mary (143), daughter of George Booth, last Earl of Warrington, was created Baron Delamere of Dunham Massey and Earl of Warrington. He died in 1819, when his son and heir, George Harry Grey, sixth Earl of Stamford, succeeded him to the titles, etc., of Warrington and Delamere. He was living in 1825, and had offspring.

It is supposed that Richard, who was the son of William Booth by his wife Elizabeth, daughter of Sir John Warburton, and was born 1570 and died 1628, was the father of Richard Booth who settled in Stratford in 1640. His daughters are mentioned in the Genealogy of the Booths of England, but the only reference made of sons is this, "That from him the Booths of Barow, in Cheshire, are descended."

Richard Booth, born in England 1607, came to America and married Elizabeth, sister of the first Joseph Hawley. His second wife's name was Mary, perhaps daughter of Robert Clark. She seems to have married second, Thomas Bennett in 1692 afterwards of Newtown.

CHILDREN OF RICHARD BOOTH.

Elizabeth, born Sept. 10th, 1641, married John Minor. Ann, born Feb. 14th, 1643. Ephriam, born Aug. 1st, 1648. Ebenezer, born Nov. 18th, 1651. John, born Nov. 5th, 1653. Joseph, born Mar. 8th, 1656. Bethia, born Aug. 18th, 1658, married the Most Worshipful Joseph Curtiss. Johanna, born Mar. 21st, 1661.

BULKLEY.

GENEALOGY OF THE BULKLEY FAMILY.

"Peter, first minister of Concord, N. H., son of Edmond Bulkley, D.D., of Odell, in the hunch of Witley, Bedfordshire; born Jan. 31st, 1583, was bred at St. John's call., Cambridge, where he proceed, A. M. 1608, and was chosen a fellow. Through favor of Lord Keeper Williams, then Bishop of Lincoln, his doceasin, he came in the Susan and Ellen, 1635; his age he then called 50; and for more perfect deception of the government spies, his wife, Grace, 33, appeared to be embarked in another ship. He first went to Cambridge, but next year to Concord, and was installed April 6th, 1637. He died Mar. 9th, 1659. His widow went to New London and died April 21st, 1669.

By 1st wife Jane, daughter of Thomas Allen, of Goldington, he had, Edmund, Mary, bap. 24th Aug., 1615. Thomas, bap. Apl. 18th, 1617. Nathaniel, 29th Nov. 1618, died at 9 years. John, bap. Feb. 17th, 1620. H. C. 1642. Mary, again Nov. 1st, 1621, died at 3 years. George, bap. May 17th, 1623. Daniel, bap. Aug. 28th, 1625. Sobey, bap. Dec. 20th 1626, died under 3 years. Probably Joseph, and one or two more. Joseph first married Martha, daughter of James Beers, of Fairfield.

By wife Grace, daughter of Sir Richard Chetewoode, Gresham, born Dec. 6th, 1636. H. C. 1655. Ebenezer, probably 1638. Dor-

NEC TEMERE : NEC TIMIDE.

Bulkley.

othy, Aug. 2nd, 1640. Peter, June 12th or Aug. 12th, 1643. His will given Genealogical Register p. 167 of 14th April 1658, in his 76th year."

"Dr. Peter, youngest son of the Rev. Peter Bulkley, D.D., married Margarete Foxcroft, of Boston, daughter of Francis Foxcroft, said to be a son of Daniel Foxcroft, Mayor of Leeds, in county York. His second wife, daughter of Gov. Danford. Dr. Peter Bulkley was an apothecary as well as a physician in Fairfield, Conn. He left but a small estate. His will is dated Mar. 25th, 1691, and he calls himself as then 49 years of age. He had, Grace, Margaret, Hannah, Sherman, Gresham and Dorothy.

Peter, son of Dr. Peter Bulkley, married Hannah, daughter of John Bulkley, son of Thomas, son of Rev. Peter Bulkley. Their children were David and Peter, bap. Mar. 9th, 1712. Sarah, bap. Dec. 14th, 1712. Sarah, Nov. 29th, 1713. Peter, bap. Oct. 9th, 1715. Andrew, bap. Oct. 6th, 1717. Gresham, bap. Aug. 13th, 1721. Sobey, bap. Oct. 4th, 1723. Olive, bap. July—1725, married James Beers. Hannah, bap. Oct. 16th, 1726. Moses, bap. July 9th, 1727. Abigail, bap. April 13th, 1729. James, bap. Aug. 3rd, 1729. Mary, Oct. 17th, 1731. Jonathan, bap. Sep. 24th, 1732." Peter Bulkley died July 5th, 1804, aged 87 years.

"Thomas, son of Rev. Peter Bulkley, married Sarah, daughter of Rev. John Jones. He with his wife and family moved from Concord to Fairfield in 1644, where he was soon afterwards granted a home—lot in the Newton Square s. w. of his brother Daniel's. He died in 1658, leaving wife Sarah, who afterwards married Anthony Wilson, of Fairfield. Mrs. Wilson in her will dated Feb. 15th, 1681, mentions Sarah, wife of Eleazer Browne, of New Haven.

NOTE—Copied from Genealogical Register at Burrough's Library, Bridgeport.

Rebecca, wife of Joseph Whelpley, of Fairfield, Hannah, John and Joseph Bulkley."

Joseph, 2nd, son of Thomas Bulkley, married Elizabeth, daughter of John Knowles, of Fairfield, and second, Martha, daughter of James Beers.

CHILDREN OF JOSEPH BULKLEY, 2ND.

Thomas, Daniel, John, Joseph; born May 9th, 1682. Peter, born May 21st, 1684. Sarah, bap. Sept. 23rd, 1694. She married Joshua Jennings. Gersham, Sept. 13th, 1696. John, March 22nd, 1702. Joseph Bulkley died intestate about 1720.

Joseph, 3rd, son of Joseph and Martha Bulkley, married Esther, daughter of Joseph Hill.

CHILDREN OF JOSEPH BULKLEY, 3RD.

Joseph, baptized March 9th, 1712. Esther, Dec. 20th, 1713. Nathan, Jan. 19, 1718, he was town recorder, and occupied his father's homestead at the time Fairfield was burned, it was probably the present homestead of Miss Hannah Hobart. Joseph, born Nov. 22nd, 1719; he is recorded as being in the Revolutionary army. Samuel, March 6th, 1726. Sarah, Feb. 23rd, 1729. Ebenezer, Dec. 5th, 1731.

Samuel, son of Joseph (3rd), married Bulah, daughter of Samuel Henry, Sept. 2nd, 1754.

CHILDREN OF SAMUEL BULKLEY.

Esther, born Dec. 7th, 1755. Samuel, born Dec. 19th, 1757. Deborah, Jan 26th, 1761. Hannah, April 4th, 1763. Mindell, Aug. 22nd, 1765. Samuel the father, died Aug. 7th, 1822.

Deborah, daughter of Samuel and Bulah Bulkley married Abel Turney; they were baptised April 16th, 1786.

CRANE.

GENEALOGY OF THE CRANE FAMILY.

ELIJAH CRANE, of Stratfield, married Abigail, daughter of Samuel Adams, of Fairfield, Conn. He died in 1726.

CHILDREN OF ELIJAH CRANE.

Abigail, baptized May 29th, 1698. Deborah, baptized April 2nd, 1699. Mary, baptized Sept. 15th, 1700. Israel, baptized March 28th, 1703. Comfort, baptized June 16th, 1706. Elijah, baptized Nov. 7th, 1708. Jabez, baptized May 9th, 1714. Abigail, baptized June 29th, 1716. Benjamin date unknown. Eunice, baptized Nov. 30th, 1740.

Abigail married Andris Trubee, of Fairfield, April 14th, 1744.

Elijah Crane (1st), entered into full communion Feb. 8th, 1697. It would seem that he had two wives, for there is a Mary Crane, who entered into full communion at the Stratfield church Oct. 22d, 1699. If such was the case he probably married his wife Abigail between the years 1703 and 1705. At this distant date it is almost impossible to definitely settle many of these statements. From the Probate Records we know that Abigail was Elijah Crane's wife before 1716.

Elijah Crane sold his place in Stratfield, March 2d, 1716, and bought a place in Fairfield April 30th, 1716, at Barlow's Plain, probably near the homestead of his father-in-law, Samuel Adams. Elijah Crane died 1726. Abigail, his wife, recognized her baptismal engagement at the Fairfield church Nov. 30th, 1740.

Elijah, son of Elijah Crane, married Elizabeth, daughter of Henry Wakelee, Aug. 3d, 1732. Jabez, their son, was baptized Feb. 17th, 1734.

Elijah (2d) and his wife entered into full communion July 29th, 1733. He died Oct., 1740. His widow married Benajah Mallory in 1743.

Curtis.

CURTISS.

DESCRIPTION OF THE CURTISS COAT OF ARMS.

According to Gillium, "Asure a fesse dancette between three ducal coronets, as is born by the name of Curtiss, and was confirmed to John Curtiss, of London, Gent., son of William Curtiss, of Hutton, in the county of Warwick, Gent., son of Eustice Curtiss, of Matisack, of said county, Gent., son of William Curtiss who was son and heir of John Curtiss, of Matisack, Gent."

This bearing was confirmed by Sir Richard at George Clarencieux, the 9th of May, 1632, and in the eighth year of the reign of Charles I.

William Curtiss came to America in the ship "Lion," 1632, and settled at Roxbury, Mass. He was the father of William and John Curtiss, who settled in Stratford, 1639. William, the father, came to this country without his family, and they followed him in 1634. He was a large land owner in Roxbury, and died there eight months after the arrival of his family.

His children were William, Thomas, Mary, John and Philip.

After his death his widow, Elizabeth, joined her two sons, William and John, in Stratford, where she died in June, 1658. The other children remained in Roxbury.

John Curtiss was born in England. He was made a freeman, in Stratford, in 1658. He died there Dec. 2nd, 1707, aged 94 years.

His wife's name was Elizabeth, by whom he had seven children. John, born Oct. 14th, 1642; Israel, born April 3rd, 1644; Elizabeth, born May 2nd, 1647; Thomas, born Jan. 14th, 1648; Joseph, born Nov. 12th, 1650; Benjamin, born Sept. 30th, 1652; Hannah, born Feb. 2nd, 1654.

The most Worshipful Joseph Curtiss, son of John and Elizabeth Curtiss, married Bethia, daughter of Richard Booth, Nov. 9th, 1676. Their children were Elizabeth, born Jan. 17th, 1677, married Samuel Uffort, 1694; Anna, born Sept. 11th, 1679; Mary, born 1681, married Joseph Nichols; Ephraim, born Dec. 31st, 1684; Joseph, born Nov. 6th, 1687; Nathan, born Feb. 21st, 1689; Josiah, born Mar. 31st, 1691; Berthia, born Mar. 10th, 1695, married Benjamin Burton; Elizer, born July 31st, 1699; Ebenezer, born Aug. 1st, 1699, died in 1700; Elizold, born Aug. 1st, 1699, died Aug. 2nd, 1699. Here we find triplets.

Joseph, second son of Joseph and Berthia Booth Curtiss, married Elizabeth, daughter of John Wells, Jr., July 5th, 1711.

"Joseph Curtiss remained near old Mill Farms, the others went to Newtown to gather grain, and on returning home were attacked by wolves so ferociously that they threw their bags of grain from the horses, and rode for home at full speed to save themselves and horses."

The Children of Joseph Curtiss, (2d), were Robert, born June 7th, 1713, died Nov. 22d, 1713; Mary, born Sept., 1714, married Daniel Curtiss; James, born Oct., 1716; Elizabeth, born Jan. 16th, 1718; Joseph, born Mar. 28th, 1721, died in 1801; Gideon, born Jan., 1722; Tabitha, born Nov., 1724, married Richard Minor, Jr.; Robert, born Aug. 13th, 1727; Bethia, born Jan., 1730, married Abraham Beardsley.

CURTISS.

Joseph Curtiss, third son of Joseph, (2d), and Elizabeth Wells Curtiss, married Martha, daughter of James Judson, Dec. 24th, 1740. She died in 1796, and he married Esther Blackman in 1797. He died 1801, aged 80 years. His children were Nehemiah, born 1740; he was a soldier in the Continental army. Joseph, born June, 1741. Phineas, born May, 1742. Abigail, born Nov. 1747. Silas, born May, 1750. Martha, born 1753, married Isaac Brooks. Judson, born Jan., 1755. Agur, born April, 1757, was also in the Continental army. Charity, born, May, 1762.

Phineas Curtiss, son of Joseph, (3d), and Elizabeth, married widow Huldah Gilbert, daughter of Samuel Judson, Feb. 23d, 1784.

CHILDREN OF PHINEAS AND HULDAH GILBERT CURTISS.

A son born, date unknown; Hepsey, born Feb. 6th, 1785, married Mr. Barteau, of Long Island. Martha, born Jan. 7th, 1787, married David Trubee, of Fairfield. Betsey, born Dec. 25th, 1788. Huldah, born, date unknown, married Aaron Turney, of Fairfield.

Betsey Curtiss, daughter of Phineas and Huldah Gilbert Curtiss, married Samuel Comfort Trubee, of Fairfield, Conn., October 22nd, 1809.

GARLICK.

GENEALOGY OF THE GARLICK OR GAIRLOCK FAMILY.

During the "Wars of the Roses," about the middle of the fifteenth century, the Garlicks or Gairlochs settled at Dinting, a township of Glossop, Derbyshire. It is supposed they came from Leeds to Dinting. The name is purely Anglo-Saxon, and was originally Gairloch, which means in the old Anglo-Saxon, a violet. The following is taken from "Historical and descriptive sketches of Glossop, England."

"At Higher Dinting was born, Master Nicholas Garlick, of respectable parents, who, after passing the days of childhood and youth there, went to teach in a school in Tidesdale, in the Peak; from thence he went accompanied by three young men, scholars of his, to Dowae College in France, where he was ordained a priest in 1582, and went to England to minister to the Catholics, who, still amid the terrors of those times, dared to follow the religion of their ancestors. He labored for some time in his native county, Derby, but was caught at last saying mass in the house of John Fitsherbert, Esq., of Derbyshire, for which offence he was tried and condemned to suffer the barbarous death of being hung, drawn and quartered."

"He suffered at Derby in the year 1588, along with Mr. Richard Ludlam and Mr. John Simpson, brother priests and fellow laborers

SAMUEL MIDDLETON GARLICK, M. D.

in the same vineyard. The following stanzas in the Sternhold and Hopkins style of poetry of those days have been preserved—written, it would appear, by one who witnessed their joy and constancy in death."

> 'When Garlick did the ladder kiss,
>   And Simpson after hie,
> Me thought that there St. Andrew was
>   Desirous for to die.'
> 'When Ludlam looked smilinglie
>   And joyful did remain,
> Me thought that there St. Stephen was
>   For to be stoned again.'

Thomas Garlick of Charlesworth was born about 1740. John Garlick, his son, married Anise Beard, and had the following children :

Thomas, an officer in the English army, came to Canada with his wife. They were shipwrecked crossing the Atlantic, and lost everything they possessed except the clothing they wore ; reaching their destination they sought to retrieve their loss. Thomas Garlick afterward received the appointment of manager of the Parliamentary Libraries, which office he retained as long as he lived. He was twice married and had several children, but it is supposed they all died before reaching middle age.

Samson, son of John and Anise Garlick, lived at Charlesworth, and died of typhus fever. Solomon, son of John and Anise Garlick, died in America. Esther, daughter of John and Anise Garlick, married James S. Middleton, came to America and died Sept., 1872, at Salem, N. H., aged about 63 years. Alice, daughter of John and Anise Garlick, married William Lewis, and died in England. Samuel, son of John and Anise Garlick, was an officer in the English army; he died at Gibralter. John, son of John and Anise Garlick, born August 2nd, 1809, married Hannah Beard, daughter of Charles Beard, of Charlesworth, England. She was born March 26th, 1811. While on a voyage to America, accompanied by her husband and children, she died of quick consumption and was buried at sea off the banks of Newfoundland, May 12th, 1848. John Garlick and his children, landed at Boston; they went immediately to visit his sister, Mrs. James Middleton, of Providence, R. I. He died at her home June 14th, 1848. He is buried in the city cemetery.

CHILDREN OF JOHN GARLICK.

Charles, born June 9th, 1832, died suddenly at Salem, N. H., Dec. 12th, 1851.

Thomas, born Nov. 6th, 1836, adopted his uncle's name, *i. e.*, Middleton. He married Clara Hovey of Salem, N. H. They had two boys, twins, who died aged 9 months.

Esther, born July 7th, 1839, died July 9th, 1861.

Samuel Middleton, born May 13th, 1845, married Harriet Trubee Knapp, daughter of Capt. Rufus and Caroline Knapp, Dec. 6th, 1877.

CHILDREN OF SAMUEL GARLICK.

Almira Elizabeth Trubee, born April 14th, 1879.
Caroline Trubee, born April 27th, 1882.
Herbert Middleton, born July 3rd, 1883.
Edward Earl, born Sept. 18th, 1884.
George Burroughs, born Nov. 16th, 1885.

MRS. FREDERICK SOMERS.
(Frances Hoile.)

GIBNEY.

ALEXANDER GIBNEY, born near Belfast, Ireland, married Mary ———, of same place.

Their son, Robert Alexander Gibney, born in Lexington, Ky., married Armando Wagley, daughter of Abraham and Mary Cassell Wagley, of Jessamine County, Kentucky.

Their son, Virgil P. Gibney, born in Lexington, Ky., married Julia A. Pendell, daughter of Edgar and Susan Alvord Trubee, of Bridgeport, Conn., June 20th, 1893. Children: Marion Pendall, born April 12th, 1894.

HOILE.

GEORGE HOILE, son of Robert Hoile, was born at Sangate England, May 3d, 1810. He came to America when about sixteen years of age and settled at Bridgeport, Conn. Afterward he removed to Fairfield, where he married Elizabeth, daughter of Samuel Comfort and Elizabeth Curtiss Trubee, April 10th, 1837. Elizabeth, his wife, died Feb. 26th, 1890, at their home in Bridgeport. He died there April 16th, 1893. They are buried in the Fairfield cemetery.

Their only child, Francis Elizabeth, married Frederick Somers, of Bridgeport, Nov. 16th, 1893.

KNAPP.

COAT OF ARMS OF THE KNAPP FAMILY.

(Norf.) Tuddenham, Needham and Warbrocke.

(Suf.) Ar, in chief three close helmets sa., in base a lion pass. of the last.

CREST.—An arm embowed in armour, ppr. garnished or, the hand of the first grasping by the blade a broken sword, or hilt and pomel of the second, with a branch of laurel verb.

MOTTO.—

THE KNAPP family were originally from Saxony, a province of Germany. By some they are regarded as Germans, by others of Saxon origin. But their early history in England leads most of the descendants to fix their nationality as Anglo-Saxon, or English.

During the fifteenth century they were people of wealth and position in Sussex County, England.

The name Knapp is derived from a Saxon word, the root of which is spelled Cnoep, signifying a summit or hill-top. John being the given name, and living on a hill, he was called John of the hill; and there being others of the same name on the hill, and said John living on the summit or knob, was called John of the Cnoep or knob. The preposition being omitted for convenience sake, he was called John Cnoep, the German formation John Knopp, and the English John Knapp. The family arms together with a full description, may be found in the Herald's College, London.

These arms were granted to Roger de Knapp, by Henry VIII., to commemorate his skill and success at a tournament held in Norfolk, England, 1540, in which he is said to have unseated three knights of great skill and bravery.

These arms are still preserved as a precious memento of worthy ancestry by the descendants of his son John.

The first of the Knapp family to come to America were William, Nicholas and Roger Knapp, who came under command of Winthrop and Salstanstall, 1630.

William, who was born in 1590, settled in Watertown, Mass. His children were William, Mary, Elizabeth, Ann, Judith, John and James. They afterwards settled in Tanton, Rosbury, Newtown, Boston and Spencer, Mass.

Nicholas Knapp settled in Watertown, Mass. By his wife, Elenora, his children were Jonathan, Smithy, Joshua, Caleb, Sarah, Ruth and Hannah. In 1648 he removed to Stamford, Conn., where by his second wife he had Moses and Lydia. Their children settled in Norwalk, Danbury, Greenwich, Rye and Peekskill.

Roger Knapp settled in New Haven and afterwards in Fairfield, where he died about 1673. His wife's name was Elizabeth. Their children were Jonathan, who died young, Elizabeth, Mary, Nathaniel, John, Roger, Lydia and Josiah.

John, son of Roger Knapp, was probably the father of Daniel Knapp, who was baptized June 21st, 1696, and Moses, baptized, date unknown. Moses is recorded as having sold a piece of land to his brother in 1720.

(Daniel and Moses are the recorded grandsons of Roger Knapp, and from evidence obtained it is more than probable that their father was John, son of Roger Knapp).

Daniel Knapp, baptized June 21st, 1696, married Abigail Banks, March 5th, 1710, and renewed covenant May 11th, 1712.

CHILDREN OF DANIEL KNAPP.

Mary, born March 7th, 1711, baptized May, 1712. John, born May 25th, 1713, baptized June 30th, 1714. Daniel, born August 14th, 1716, baptized Sept. 2d, 1716. Abigail, born Dec. 20th, 1719, baptized March 1st, 1720. Ann, born July 11th, 1721, baptized Aug. 20th, 1721. Ellen, born May 24th, 1724. Sarah, born May 26th, 1726. Joseph, born July 20th, 1731. Elizabeth, born Sept. 27th, 1736, died Sept. 27th, 1755.

John Knapp, son of Daniel and Abigail Banks Knapp, covenanted Nov. 4th, 1737; he married Hannah, daughter of Mr. Mathew Jennings, June 29th, 1738.

CHILDREN OF JOHN KNAPP, 1ST.

James, born July 7th, 1739. Nehemiah, born Nov. 9th, 1741. Hannah, born June 2nd, 1844. Amos, born June 2nd, 1744. John, born March 24th, 1753. Abigail, born March 3rd, 1754.

John Knapp, son of John and Hannah, married Mary Wilson of Fairfield Woods. They were baptized Feb. 1st, 1787.

On May 15th, 1775, John Knapp enlisted in the Fifth Regiment, and Fourth Company of the Continental Army, under the command of Colonel Waterbury, and Capt. Dimon, of Fairfield. John Knapp was at that time twenty-three years of age. He marched with his company during the inclemency of the winter season, from Boston to New York. The gun which our ancestor carried during this campaign is still in existence. On Dec. 5th, 1775, he was honorably discharged from service, and probably re-enlisted in 1776, and was commissioned a lieutenant.

CHILDREN OF JOHN KNAPP, 2ND.

Mary, baptized at the house of Nathaniel Wilson, at a lecture, Feb. 1st, 1787. Ruth, baptized Feb. 1st, 1787, married Abel Jennings. Hannah, married Andrew Turney, they had ten children. Anna, married Levi Turney. John, born June, 1797. Sarah, married Capt. Ephriam Knapp, who kept a Hotel in Bridgeport. Polly, married John Brown. Wilson, married Maria Meeker.

Capt. John Knapp, son of Capt. John and Mary Wilson Knapp, married Esther, daughter of Abel and Deborah Buckley Turney, 1811. He died Oct. 28th, 1872, aged 85 years, 10 months and 26 days. Esther, his wife, died September 7th, 1878. She was a member of the Congregational church in Fairfield. They are buried in the Fairfield cemetery.

CHILDREN OF JOHN KNAPP, 3RD.

Eliza Ann, born May 18th, 1812, married William Trubee, son of Samuel Comfort and Elizabeth Curtis Trubee, July 30th, 1836. Rufus, born Dec. 7th, 1813. John, born June 22nd, 1816, married 1st, Mary Wilson, who was born June 29th, 1823, and died April 1st, 1852. Their children were Jane, Cornelia and Charles. He married 2nd, Mary Alvord of Southport. She was born Dec. 29th,

1823; died, 1887. He died Sept. 4th, 1884. William, son of John and Esther Knapp, was born Feb. 21st, 1825.

Henry Knapp, youngest child of John and Mary Wilson Knapp, married Sarah Peet. Their children were Edward, Richard, and daughter Ella.

Mary Knapp married Alfred Hubbell. They had one daughter, Suesan Esther, who married Mr. Reynolds of Bridgeport.

Capt. Rufus Knapp, son of Capt. John and Esther Knapp, married Caroline, daughter of Samuel Comfort and Elizabeth Curtis Trubee, Oct. 28th, 1840.

He was commander of the passenger ship "Leviathan," and was lost with it during the voyage from New York to Liverpool, Nov. 1853. As nothing has ever been heard of the ship it is supposed she foundered and went down in mid-ocean with all on board.

Caroline, his wife, died Jan. 25th, 1882.

CHILDREN OF CAPT. RUFUS KNAPP.

Emily Dodge, Caroline, Rufus Clifton.

Harriet Trubee, born Jan. 3rd, 1848, married Samuel Middleton Garlick, Dec. 6th, 1877. Charles Ansel, born Jan. 28th, 1850; died Aug. 31st, 1851. Herbert Merton, youngest son.

Rufus Clifton, son of Capt. Rufus and Caroline Trubee Knapp, married Esther Holmes, daughter of Jarrat Morford of Bridgeport, July 21st, 1870. Esther, his wife, died —— 1881.

CHILDREN OF RUFUS KNAPP, 2ND.

Maria Morford, born July 7th, 1871; died Jan. 11th, 1882. His wife and child are buried in Mountain Grove Cemetery.

RUFUS CLIFTON KNAPP.

Capt. William Knapp, son of Capt. John and Esther Turney Knapp, married Harriet, daughter of Samuel Comfort and Elizabeth Curtis Trubee, July 11th, 1849. He was captain of the ship "Evening Star," and was lost with it during a cyclone, Oct. 3rd, 1866, 180 miles east of Tybee When convinced that the steamer would founder, Capt. Knapp, who had made every effort to save her, said—"If I am lost tell them at home I died doing my duty."

CHILDREN OF CAPT. WILLIAM KNAPP.

Isabelle Trubee, born Jan. 19th, 1852, married George Sanford, Oct. 31st, 1883.

Elizabeth Curtis, born Oct. 22nd, 1855, married Dr. John Winthrop Wright, Dec. 9th, 1885.

Virginia, married Arthur Wesley Perry, April 6th, 1881. A twin sister to Virginia died at birth.

Lena, youngest daughter, married Charles Bibbons Bennett, Feb. 19th, 1889.

MILLER.

In December, 1835, Zepheniah Miller, of Fairfield, formerly of Bedford, Conn., married Jane Ann, daughter of David and Martha Curtiss Trubee. She died May 8th, 1882. He died June 4th, 1888. They are buried in the Fairfield cemetery. They had one child, Arthur Miles, born June 24th, 1837.

On July 31st, 1866, Arthur Miles, son of Zepheniah and Jane Ann Trubee Miller, married Susan, daughter of the late Elihu and Cornelia Turney Sanford. He died April 15th, 1892, and is buried in the Fairfield cemetery. They had two children, Arthur Sanford Miller and Hattie Sanford Miller.

PERRY.

On April 6th, 1881, Arthur Wesley Perry, youngest son of Curtiss and Harriett Perry, married Virginia Knapp, daughter of William and Harriet Trubee Knapp, of Fairfield. Virginia, wife of Arthur Perry died June 8th, 1894.

CHILDREN OF ARTHUR WESLEY PERRY.

Hazel Trubee, born, April 13th, 1882. William Knapp, born April 29th, 1884; died 1887. Curtiss Perry, born April 29th, 1884; died April 29th, 1884. Maud Harriett, born Nov. 16th, 1886. Julian Wesley, born Feb. 2nd, 1892.

ARTHUR MILLS MILLER.

FREDERICK SOMERS.

SANFORD.

Elihu Sanford, of New Haven, married Cornelia, daughter of Stephen and Ruthie Buddington Turney, of Fairfield.

CHILDREN OF ELIHU SANFORD.

Elihu, Cornelia, Elizabeth, Susan, Stephen, George, Hattie.

On October 31st, 1883, George, son of the late Elihu and Cornelia Turney Sanford, married Isabella, daughter of William and Harriett Trubee Knapp, of Fairfield.

SOMERS.

Frederick Somers was born at Flowery-field, Cheshire, England, January 3d, 1845. His father died in 1847. His mother was born at Hyde, Cheshire, England, in 1821; was married to Benjamin Hatfield, of Flowery-field, Cheshire, England, in 1853; came to America and settled in Providence, R. I., in 1854.

Frederick Somers came to Bridgeport, Conn., in 1875; retired from business in 1893; was married to Francis E. Hoile, daughter of the late George and Elizabeth Hoile, by the Rev. Charles Ray Palmer, pastor of the North Congregational Church, Bridgeport, Conn., November 16th, 1893.

TURNEY.

GENEALOGY OF THE TURNEYS OF FAIRFIELD.

Benjamin Turney came from Concord, Mass., where he was made freeman, June 2nd, 1641. His wife's name was Mary. They had three children born at Concord, the others in Fairfield. They were Mary, born 1631. Robert, born 1633. Judith, born 1635. Ann, born 1637. Rebecca, Sarah, Ruth and Benjamin. Benjamin (1st) became a large land owner in Fairfield, and died there 1648. His widow married Joseph Middlebrook, who also came from Concord to Fairfield.

Mary Turney, daughter of Benjamin and Mary Turney, married Nathaniel Seeley.

Rebecca Turney, married Stephen Sherwood of Greenwich.

Capt. Robert Turney married Elizabeth, daughter of Samuel Wilson, and settled at Pequonnock.

CHILDREN OF CAPT. ROBERT TURNEY.

Abagail, born Feb. 25th, 1661. Sarah, born Sept. 25th, 1663. Elizabeth, born July 15th, 1668. Rebecca, born July 10th, 1671. Robert, Benjamin, Mary, Ruth, Martha, Thomas and Rebecca were baptized Jan. 27th, 1695.

Capt. Robert died before 1690, as his will was probated at that time. He was also a large land owner.

ZEPHENIAH MILLER.

Robert Turney, son of Captain Robert and Elizabeth Wilson Turney, married Rebecca ———, and renewed covenant January 18th, 1713.

CHILDREN OF ROBERT TURNEY, 2ND.

Abagail, baptized April 10th, 1707. John, baptized May 22nd, 1709. Deborah, baptized Jan. 1711. She married James Burr. Mary, baptized Oct. 26th, 1712. Jerusha, baptized May 17th, 1713. John, baptized March 31st, 1714. Stephen, baptized May 28th, 1721.

These children must have been baptized by the Rev. Joseph Webb, who died Tuesday evening at nine o'clock, 1732, at Unity, now Trumbull, and was brought home and buried the following day.

Stephen Turney, son of Robert and Rebecca Turney, married Sarah Squires, Dec. 17th, 1748.

CHILDREN OF STEPHEN TURNEY.

David, baptized Dec. 10th, 1748. Samuel, baptized June 10th, 1750. Aaron, baptized April 12th, 1752. Aaron, baptized July 7th, 1754. Peter, baptized Jan. 6th, 1756. Asa, baptized Oct. 1st, 1759. Abel, baptized Oct. 3rd, 1762. Joab, baptized Nov. 24th, 1765.

Sarah, wife of Stephen Turney, died Jan. 4th, 1768, aged about 56 years. Stephen's second wife's name was Alvira, by whom he had Elijah, baptized Mar. 7th, 1777. Joel, baptized June 22nd, —. They were baptized in the old Meeting House, by Rev. Mr. Dickinson, before it was burned by the British. Stephen Turney died Jan. 26th, 1786, aged 69 years.

Capt. Aaron Turney, who bravely helped to defend the fort at Grover's Hill, was son of Stephen and Sarah Squires Turney. He married, first, Sarah, daughter of Thomas and Hannah Staples, Jan. 26th, 1782; second, Ellen Burr Gold, who was the daughter of Capt. Abel and Ellen Burr Gold. She was born July 23rd, 1761; married, first, Capt. Samuel Squire (his third wife); second, Lieut. Israel Chapman; third, Capt. Aaron Turney. She received pensions from her three husbands, for they had all fought bravely in the Revolutionary war. She died Oct. 1st, 1845.

CHILDREN OF AARON TURNEY.

Squire, baptized April 20th, 1783. Stephen, baptized June 18th, 1786, died 1787, aged 1 year. Stephen, baptized June 22nd, 1788. Jesse, baptized June 12th, 1791. Sarah, baptized Feb., 1792. Cyrus, date unknown. Sarah, born Dec. 16th, 1799.

Stephen Turney married Ruth Biddington. Jesse married Huldah Curtis. Cyrus married Mary Stowe. Sarah married Andrew Trubee, Jan. 12th, 1823.

Abel Turney, son of Stephen and Sarah Squires Turney, married Deborah Burkley; they were baptized April 16th, 1786, by the Rev. Noah Hobart.

THEIR CHILDREN.

Ellen, baptized in private (the mother being dangerously ill), June 2nd, 1789. Levi, baptized June 12th, 1791, married Anne Knapp. Esther, baptized June 23rd, 1793, married John Knapp, Jr., 1810. Samuel, baptized Oct. 17th, 1795. Mary, baptized in private (being dangerously ill), Sept. 19th, 1797. Hannah, born about 1799, died at Fairfield, 1891. Andrew, date of birth unknown, married Hannah, daughter of John Knapp, Jr., and had a large family of children; some of them still living in Fairfield, are among its best citizens. Abel, date of birth unknown. Wilson married Caroline McKenzie.

MRS. ZEPHENIAH MILLER.
(JANE ANN TRUBEE.)

TRUBEE.

GENEALOGY OF THE TRUBEE OR TRUBY FAMILY.

ANDRIS TRUBEE came from Holland to America in the latter part of 1600 or early in 1700, and settled in Boston ; later he removed to Fairfield, Conn., and established a store.

He was twice married. His first wife's name was probably Abigail, by whom he had a daughter, Eunice, born July 11th, 1740.

He married his second wife, Abigail, daughter of Elijah and Abigail Adams Crane, April 14th, 1744. He died in 1758, and his wife died in 1760.

CHILDREN OF ANDRIS TRUBEE.

Samuel Cohen, born, 1744. Getto, (a daughter), born January 27th, 1746, died October 18th, 1748. Ansel, born May 18th, 1747. Alexander, born October 27th, 1748. Gerlow, (a daughter), baptized October 18th, 1748. David, born December 22nd, 1750. Comfort, born November 9th, 1754. Esther, born February 23rd, 1758.

Ansel Trubee, son of Andris and Abigail Trubee, married Isabelle Beers December 15th, 1769. He was a communicant in 1822, and died in a fit December 26th, 1823. His wife, Isabelle, died in Fairfield, March 16th, 1836.

CHILDREN OF ANSEL TRUBEE.

Abigail, born, 1770. Eunice, born March 1st, 1773. Sarah, born August 6th, 1776. David, born November 9th, 1778, was confirmed

October 18th, 1798. Esther, born July 13th, 1781. Ansel, born July 13th, 1781. Samuel Comfort, born December 7th, 1787. William, baptized October 14th, 1787. Jerusha, date of birth unknown. Andrew, born August 16th, 1790.

Abigail Trubee was married to Ebenezer Platt, of Reading, Conn., December 8th, 1789, by Rev. Andrew Elliott. They moved to New York State, and all trace of them was lost.

Eunice Trubee was married to Ezra Knapp March 27th, 1795, by Rev. Mr. Shelton, for which he received 12 shillings. They had two children, Ezra Morehouse, baptized October 30th, 1796. George baptized May 12th, 1799. Ezra Knapp died and Eunice married for her second husband, Joseph White, of Greenfield Hill, Conn. Ezra, her son, died 1834, aged 38 years. Eunice White died 1836, during the absence of her husband, and was found by him upon his return home from work at noon. Her remains lie buried by the side of her son and second husband in the Greenfield cemetery.

Sarah Trubee, (called Sallie), was confirmed October 18th, 1798, and married Samuel, son of Thomas Staples, May, 1817. She died July 9th, 1847, aged 71 years.

Esther Trubee married Mr. Neffis, of Troy, N. Y., and had two daughters. The elder, a woman of remarkable ability, married Mr. Curtiss, of Rochester. They had three daughters who married, but all died before reaching middle age. Julia, the second daughter of Esther and Mr. Neffis, was said to be beautiful. She married Dr. Harral, of New Orleans, brother of Mr. Harral, of Bridgeport, Conn. They had one daughter who died in her youth.

Jerusha Trubee married Lorenzo Crow. Their history and place of residence is unknown.

CHARLOTTE TRUBEE.

David Trubee, son of Ansel and Isabelle Beers Trubee, married Charlotte Parrott, March 20th, 1804. I find in the old Records of the Congregational Church of Fairfield, that Charlotte Parrott professing faith in Christ, and obedience to him, was baptized by Dr. Burranth, January 26th, 1806. David and Charlotte Trubee had a daughter, Rebecca, who was baptized February 14th, 1807, and died February 20th, 1807. Charlotte, died February 28th, 1807, aged 21 years. David then married Martha Curtiss, daughter of Phineas and Huldah Curtiss, of Stratford, November 20th, 1808. He paid 12 shillings to Rev. Mr. Shelton for performing the ceremony.

THE CHILDREN OF DAVID AND MARTHA CURTIS TRUBEE.

Charlotte, born Aug. 10th, 1810, was baptized Sept. 30th, 1810, and died at Bridgeport, Feb. 20th, 1875. Jane Ann, born Jan. 1st, 1816, was baptized July 21st, 1816, and married Zephemah Miller, of Fairfield, December, 1835. She died May 8th, 1882. Martha (2nd), wife of David Trubee, died Oct. 28th, 1859. David Trubee died March 2nd, 1866. His first wife and child are buried in the old Fairfield cemetery; the others are buried in the new cemetery.

Samuel Comfort Trubee, son of Ansel and Isabella Trubee, married Elizabeth Curtiss, daughter of Phineas and Huldah Curtiss, at Fairfield, October 22nd, 1809. Elizabeth, his wife, was born in Stratford, Conn., Dec. 25th, 1788. She died Sept. 17th, 1879, aged 90 years, 8 months and 26 days. Samuel Comfort died at Fairfield, Sept. 18th, 1871. They are buried in the Fairfield cemetery.

CHILDREN OF SAMUEL COMFORT TRUBEE.

Samuel Curtiss, born Aug. 30th, 1810, was baptized Sept. 30th, 1810. William, born May 13th, 1813. Elizabeth, born Sept. 25th,

1815, married George Hoile, April 10th, 1837. She died Feb. 26th, 1890. He died April 16th, 1893. Caroline, born Jan. 6th, 1819, married Capt. Rufus Knapp, Oct. 28th, 1840. Capt. Knapp was lost at sea in the winter of 1853. Caroline, his wife, died Feb. ——, 1882. Harriett, born April 17th, 1823, married Capt. William Knapp, July 11th, 1849. Capt. William was lost at sea, Oct. 3rd, 1866. David, born Sept. 25th, 1825.

Samuel Curtiss Trubee, son of Samuel Comfort and Elizabeth Curtiss Trubee, married Clarissa Brown Miller, daughter of Benajah and Sarah Conklin Miller, Jan. 3rd, 1836. She was born Dec. 23rd, 1813; died, Feb. 8th, 1839. Samuel Curtiss Trubee married for his second wife, Amy Almira Lord, daughter of Benjamin and Dorcus Minor Lord of Lyme, Conn., Sept. 3rd, 1840.

CHILDREN OF SAMUEL CURTISS AND ALMIRA TRUBEE.

Samuel Lord, born Dec. 11th, 1842, at Shelter Island, N. Y.; died suddenly at Bridgeport, Conn., of malignant croup, Dec. 9th, 1848, aged 5 years, 7 months and 8 days.

Almira Lord, born Aug. 19th, 1844; died of scarlet fever at Bridgeport, Mar. 25th, 1852, aged 7 years, 7 months and 6 days.

"They were lovely and pleasant in their lives, and in their death they were not divided."

Amy Almira, wife of Samuel Curtiss Trubee, died Jan. 22nd, 1879, aged 68 years, 8 months and 10 days.

Samuel Curtiss Trubee was married to Mary Caroline, daughter of Isaiah and Caroline Terry of Wading River, L. I., August 4th, 1880.

William Trubee, son of Samuel Comfort and Elizabeth Curtiss Trubee, married Eliza Ann Knapp, daughter of Capt. John and

WILLIAM ALVORD TRUBEE.

Esther Turney Knapp of Holland Heights, Fairfield, July 30th, 1836. He died Feb. 2nd, 1881, and is buried in the Fairfield cemetery.

CHILDREN OF WILLIAM AND ELIZA KNAPP.

William Edgar, born July 27th, 1837. Rufus, born June 17th, 1839; died Jan. 9th, 1843. Samuel Curtiss, born July 17th, 1842. Frederick, born April 3rd, 1843.

William Edgar Trubee, son of William and Eliza Ann Trubee, married Susan Curtiss Alvord, Jan. 10th, 1860. She was the daughter of Jessup and Susan Curtiss Alvord of Southport, Conn. Jessup Alvord was born at Hull's Farms; his wife Susan was born in Stratford. William Edgar Trubee died Dec. 5th, 1890, at Bridgeport, Conn., and is buried at Mountain Grove cemetery.

CHILDREN OF WILLIAM E. AND SUSAN A. TRUBEE.

Susie Alvord, born March 30th, 1862; died Oct. 1865, and is buried at Fairfield.

Jessie Alvord, born March 3rd, 1864, married Henry Alfred Bishop, Feb. 6th, 1883.

William Alvord, born March 22nd, 1867.

Julia Alvord, born June 30th, 1869, married Dr. Virgil P. Gibney of New York City, June 20th, 1893.

William Alvord Trubee, son of William Edgar and Susan Alvord Trubee, married Ann J. Rice, daughter of Dr. Rice of Lockport, N. Y., Sept. 10th, 1890.

CHILDREN OF WILLIAM A. AND ANN TRUBEE.

William Edgar, born Dec. 4th, 1891.

Samuel Curtiss Trubee, son of William and Eliza Ann Trubee, married Ada Alden of Westport, Conn.

CHILDREN OF SAMUEL CURTISS, 2ND, AND ADA TRUBEE.

Grace, born May 18th, 1869; died Sept. 28th, 1893.

Frank Curtiss, born Oct. 3rd, 1870, married April 11th, 1894, Elizabeth, daughter of Mrs. John Martin Henderson of Elizabeth, New Jersey.

Frederick Trubee, son of William and Eliza Ann Trubee, married Mary Waterman Baldwin, daughter of Samuel Baldwin of Bridgeport, Oct. 29th, 1868.

CHILDREN OF FREDERICK AND MARY BALDWIN TRUBEE.

Mary Kate, born Feb. 2nd, 1871, married Harry Davison of New York City, April 13th, 1893.

Alice Bussey, born Nov. 16th, 1872.

On Dec. 15th, 1848, David, youngest child of Samuel Comfort and Elizabeth Curtiss Trubee, married Susan, daughter of Capt. Elisha and Susan Gifford Doane, of Cape Cod, Mass. Susan Gifford's father was a descendant of Lord De Gifford, who fought under Richard Coeur De Lion during the war of the Crusades. Her mother was a descendant of Lord Broadbrook, who came to America before the Revolution and settled at Cape Cod, Mass. Mrs. Elisha Doane was a lady of noble presence and dignified manner; she possessed those traits of character which caused her to be respected, admired and beloved, not only by her own family, but by all with whom she came in contact.

Andrew Trubee, son of Ansel and Isabella Trubee, married Sallie, daughter of Captain Aaron Turney of Fairfield, Conn., Jan. 12th, 1823.

SAMUEL CURTISS TRUBEE.

FRANK TRUBEE.

TRUBEE.

CHILDREN OF ANDREW AND SARAH TRUBEE.

Sarah Elizabeth, born Oct. 29th, 1828, married James Staples of Bridgeport, Conn., formerly of Swanville, Maine, Sept. 21st, 1858.

Francis Louisa, born Nov. 14th, 1836; died Sept. 17th, 1849.

Sarah, wife of Andrew Trubee, died Dec. 8th, 1868.

Andrew Trubee, died Nov. 11th, 1875.

STAPLES.

GENEALOGY OF THE STAPLES FAMILY.

Staples was originally Staple, the name being given to the manufacturer of a staple product. Three brothers of that name, Peter, Thomas and third unknown, came from England to that part of Massachusetts in 1640, now Kittery, Maine. Peter remained there and Thomas removed to Connecticut. Kittery records said "went West" and settled at Fairfield, Conn. The third brother, whose name is unknown, removed to Virginia.

Miles Staples, great grandson of Peter, married Sarah Trefethern, June 11th, 1753. The ceremony being performed by the Rev. Benjamin Stevens. They settled at Prospect, Maine.

Miles, son of Miles and Sarah Trefethern Staples, moved to Swanville and married.

CHILDREN OF MILES STAPLES.

Hezekiah, born March 24th, 1792. Anna, Josiah, Miles, Joseph, Mary Jane, Aaron, Ruben, George, Alfred.

Hezekiah Staples married Elizabeth Treat. She was born Sept. 1st, 1792.

CHILDREN OF HEZEKIAH AND ELIZABETH STAPLES.

Maria, born Dec. 30th, 1816. Aaron, born Nov. 4th, 1818; died Sept. 5th, 1819. Hezekiah, Jr., born Jan. 1st, 1820, became mas-

FRANK T. STAPLES.

ter of the brig "J. W. Godfrey," which sailed from Florida, Dec. 27th, 1852, and was lost at sea during the voyage home. Lydia T., born May 8th, 1821. Richard T., born July 5th, 1822, was a passenger on the brig "J. W. Godfrey," and was lost with it. James, born Jan. 19th, 1824. Samuel, born June 22nd, 1826; died March 18th, 1827. Josiah S., born Sept. 1st, 1827, became master of the brig "Mariel," and was lost with it on Cohassett Ledge, April 6th, 1852. Elizabeth Ann, born Sept. 4th, 1830. Mary Armanda, born Oct. 2nd, 1831; died July 13th, 1865. Samuel M., born Aug. 3, 1833; died at the West Indies, Oct. 7th, 1852. George Andrew, born Feb. 13th, 1837.

James Staples, son of Hezekiah and Elizabeth Staples of Swanville, Me., married his second wife, Sarah Elizabeth, daughter of Andrew and Sarah Turney Trubee of East Bridgeport, Sept. 21st, 1858.

CHILDREN OF JAMES AND SARAH STAPLES.

Frank Trubee, born Nov. 24th, 1863, married Laura Francis Stevens, Dec. 16th, 1884. She is the only child of the late William and Mary C. Stevens of East Bridgeport, and was born Oct. 18th, 1863.

CHILDREN OF FRANK AND LAURA STAPLES.

Richard Trubee, born Sept. 4th, 1885.

GENEALOGY OF THE STAPLES FAMILY OF FAIRFIELD, CONN.

Thomas, the brother of Peter Staples of Kittery, Me., was one of the first settlers of Fairfield. He came to Fairfield about 1650. His home lot was on the north side of Ludlow square. He was a large land owner. By his wife, Mary, he had Mary, who was the second wife of Josiah Harvey. Hannah married John Beach.

Mahetable, who probably married Jonathan Fenton. Thomas and John. Thomas Staples, 1st, died before 1688.

Thomas Staples, son of Thomas and Mary Staples, married Deborah ——.

CHILDREN OF THOMAS, 2ND, AND DEBORAH STAPLES.

Thomas, baptized Sept. 14th, 1701, entered into full communion under Rev. Joseph Webb, July 6th, 1712. Samuel, baptized May 30th, 1708.

Thomas Staples, (3rd), married Deborah. They were baptized 1735 ; renewed covenant, July 5th, 1738.

CHILDREN OF THOMAS, 3RD, AND DEBORAH STAPLES.

John, born Oct. 23rd, 1737, married Jessie Hunt, March 22nd, 1753. Sarah, born June 18th, 1732. Ruhamah, born June 17th, 1739. (Sambo, a negro child living with Thomas Staples 3rd, was baptized Aug. 18th, 1839). Hannah, born 1740; died July 24th, 1801. Samuel, baptized March 6th, 1741. Mary, baptized Oct. 24th, 1742. Ruhamah, baptized June 10th, 1748.

Thomas Staples, (4th), and Hannah, his wife, were baptized Mar. 7th, 1777, and entered into full communion, May 4th, 1777.

CHILDREN OF THOMAS, 4TH, AND HANNAH STAPLES.

Walter was baptized in private on account of an alarm from a British fleet which came up near the town, and this family was about to disperse, Mar. 7th, 1777. Thomas, aged 16 years, professing faith in Christ and obedience to Him, was baptized Mar. 7th, 1777. Sarah, aged 14 years, was baptized, professing faith in Christ and obedience to Him, Mar. 7th, 1777. She married Aaron Turney. Samuel was baptized Mar. 7th, 1777.

The above baptisms were administered in the Meeting House, afterwards burned by the British.

Samuel Staples, son of Thomas and Hannah, married Esther Parsons, June 16th, 1791. She died Nov. 4th, 1815, in the 43rd year of her age. Samuel married for his second wife, Sallie, daughter of Ansel Trubee of Fairfield, May 1817. He died Feb. 29th, 1825, aged 62 years. Sallie, his wife, died 1847, aged 71 years.

WELLS.

"Welles, Governor Thomas, of Connecticut, was born in Essex County, England, in the year 1598, and came from Northamptonshire, England, to America, in 1636." 'In the English calendar of Colonnial State Papers is found the following: 1635, Record Commission State Papers.' 'Thomas Welles and Elizabeth, his wife, recusant (that is nonconformist) in Rothwell, Northamptonshire.' As he disappeared from Rothwell in 1635, and having lost all his property by confiscation, he doubtless at that time entered the service of Lord Saye and Sele as private secretary, and came to America early in the spring of 1636. "Recusant signifies the refusal to subscribe to the oath of conformity to the Established Church of England, which requires the acknowledgement of the King as head of the church, instead of the Pope. The Puritans would not subscribe on oath to either, and hence their emigration. Thomas Wells was secretary of Lord Saye, and the families were undoubtedly connected."

"Thomas Wells was chosen as magistrate of the Colony of Connecticut in 1637, which office he held every successive year until his decease in 1659-60, a period of twenty-two years. Besides holding other offices, he was elected Deputy Governor in 1654, and Governor of Connecticut Colony in 1655, and in 1656–57 Deputy Governor; in 1658 Governor, and in 1659 Deputy Governor, which

WELLS.

position he held at his death, Jan. 14th, 1659-60. He married his first wife—a Miss Hunt—in England, she being the mother of all his children. He married second, in Wetherfield, about 1646, Elizabeth Foote, a daughter of John Deming, of England. She died July 28th, 1683."

CHILDREN OF THOMAS WELLS.

Ann, born about 1619.
John, born about 1621.
Robert, born about 1624.
Thomas, born about 1627.
Samuel, born about 1630.
Sarah, born about 1632.
Mary, born about 1634.
Joseph, born about 1637.

John, son of Governor Thomas Wells, came to America with his father in 1636, landed at Saybrook, came thence to Hartford in the autumn of 1636, and to Stratford in 1645 (says the history of the Wells family), where he resided until his death. He was made freeman of Hartford, April 1st, 1645. He was elected representative from Stratford in 1656-57 and 59. In 1658 he was elected Magistrate of Stratford and Judge of Probate, according to the following : 'March, 1858. This Court doth appoint Mr. Ward, Mr. Hill, with the Townsmen of Fairfield, to assist Mr. John Wells in procuring wills and taking in inventories, and distributing estates of persons that die intestate, and to appoint administrators, and in case any one unsatisfied with their determinations herein, they have liberty to take their address to ye next session of this court. This order respects Stratford, Fairfield and Norwalk.'

"John Wells married in Stratford, Elizabeth Bourne, a young woman who came to New England with Arthur Bostwick." His will was dated Oct. 19th, 1659, and he died soon after, as he was deceased when his father died the next January. In his will he says, 'I give to my beloved wife, Elizabeth Wells, all that is due to her in England, and £40 to carry with her if she please to go to England.' "He also gave his son, Robert, to his father, to be educated; and, although the grandfather died a little more than two months after, Robert went to Wetherfield and lived and died there, receiving a considerable portion of his grandfather's estate.

John, 2nd, son of John, 1st, and Elizabeth Bourne Wells, married Mary, daughter of John Hollister. He died March 24th, 1713-14. They had eight children. Elizabeth, their daughter, married Joseph Curtiss, Jr., son of Joseph, 1st, and Bethia Booth Curtiss, July 5th, 1711.

NOTE.—The account of the ancestry of the Wells family is voluminous and satisfactory. The family is of ancient origin (794) and of high rank in Normandy and England, with royal intermarriages, for over seven centuries. Gov. Thomas Wells was a lineal descendent of the Essex branch of the Wells family in England. He came to America in 1636 with his kinsman, Lord Saye and Sele. The estate, where his family lived, was known for centuries as Rayne Hall. Gov. Thomas Wells was married in England, 1618, to a Miss Hunt, who was of a highly respectable family. The Wells coat of arms is very handsome.

JOHN WINTHROP WRIGHT, M. D.

WRIGHT.

Leverett Wright of Cromwell, Conn., married Lucy Smith.

CHILDREN OF LEVERETT AND LUCY WRIGHT.

John Winthrop, born June 8th, 1852.
Wallace, Berton.

John Winthrop Wright, M. D., married Elizabeth Curtiss Knapp, daughter of William and Harriet Trubee Knapp of Fairfield, Dec. 8th, 1885.

CHILDREN OF JOHN WINTHROP WRIGHT, M. D.

Lucy, daughter of J. W. Wright, by his first wife.
Elizabeth Curtiss, born Jan. 11th, 1887.
William Winthrop, born Dec. 2nd, 1888.
Marion, born Mar. 3rd, 1893.

NOTES.

We are indebted to Miss Martha Beach for the artistic copies of the coast-of-arms which add so much to the value of this family history.

The property west of Hyde's Pond which was originally owned by Edward Adams, of Fairfield, and inherited by Mrs. Zepheniah Miller and Miss Charlotte Trubee, was sold by them. PAGES 19 and 128

Abel Turney received his pension by Act of Congress of 1832. He served in the Continental Army for two years during the War of the American Revolution. PAGE 132

Joseph Livesley, of Fairfield, had two daughters; they married two brothers, David and Joseph Beers, of Fairfield, Conn. PAGE 29

Mr. Stephen Barteau, of Fire Place, Long Island, married Hepzibah, daughter of Phineas and Huldah Curtiss, of Stratford, Conn. PAGE 117

Mr. Gold, to whom reference is made upon this page, was Mr. Nathan Gold, Jr., son of Major Nathan Gold, of Fairfield. He was Lieutenant and Deputy Governor of the Colony of Connecticut for many years. He died Oct. 3rd, 1723. PAGE 14

Ætatis Suae, 60.

PAGE 47 The house referred to is now in the possession of the writer. It was built by Captain Fowler about 1784, upon the same site where formerly stood the parsonage of Rev. Mr. Elliott, which was burned by the British July 7th. 1779.

PAGE 35 Dr. George Harral was the son of Dr. George Harral, who first practiced medicine at Rochester, N. Y., afterwards at Charleston, S. C.

Dr. George Harral, Jr., married for his second wife, Julia Neffis, daughter of Mr. and Mrs. Esther Trubee Neffis, of Rochester, N. Y., and niece of Samuel Comfort Trubee, of Fairfield, Conn. After Dr. and Mrs. George Harral's marriage they resided at New Orleans, where in the practice of his profession he acquired great reputation for skill in surgery. An only daughter, Mary, inherited her mother's beauty. She died on her way north, of malarial fever.

Dr. George Harral, Jr., was brother of the late Mr. Henry Harral, of Bridgeport, Conn.

PAGE 86 Goody Knapp's place of execution was not on the hill as stated on this page; the writer was misinformed as to this location. Coming into possession of a map of the early settlers of Pequonnock, we find that Goody Knapp was hung, probably, upon the hill now called Spooner's Park; for her place of execution was on property belonging to one Michael Fry, whose mill was near the eastern border of the settlement. The remains of an old mill dam can still be seen by the stream at the foot of the above mentioned hill. The Indian fields was that large tract of level land now known as Spooner's farm. Her place of execution was northwest of this field.

PAGE 44 The physician referred to was Dr. David Hull, who practiced medicine for many years at Fairfield, Conn., and died there at the age of 75 years.

ERRATA.

Page 117.

Huldah, daughter of Phineas and Huldah Curtiss, married Jesse, son of Aaron Turney of Fairfield, Conn.

Page 121.—GIBNEY.

Virgil P. Gibney, born in Lexington, Ky., married Julia A., daughter of Edgar and Susan Alvord Trubee of Bridgeport, Conn., June 20th, 1893. Children:—Marion Pendell, born April 12th, 1894.

Page 126.

Children of Captain Rufus Knapp: Emily Dodge, Caroline Clifton, Rufus Clifton.

Page 132.

Abel Turney, son of Stephen and Sarah Turney, married Deborah, daughter of Samuel and Bulah Bulkley.

Page 136.

Caroline, wife of Captain Rufus Knapp, died Jan. 25th, 1882.

Page 136.

Samuel Lord Trubee, died, aged 5 years, 11 months and 8 days.

Page 147.—WRIGHT.

William Winthrop Wright, born Dec. 2nd, 1889.

www.ingramcontent.com/pod-product-compliance
Lightning Source LLC
Chambersburg PA
CBHW021812230426
43669CB00008B/726